SWAG

by

Joe Roseman

**Grosvenor House
Publishing Limited**

This book is published by
Grosvenor House Publishing Ltd
28-30 High Street, Guildford, Surrey, GU1 3EL.
www.grosvenorhousepublishing.co.uk

A CIP record for this book
is available from the British Library

ISBN 978-1-78148-518-7

For Gerald

Contents

Foreword by Louis Bacon, Founder of Moore Capital Management

Joe started working for me in 1994 amidst one of the worst bear markets for fixed income in memory. He was originally based from the Moore Capital office in Paris, and was mainly responsible for the execution of the firm's European fixed income trades. Portfolio Managers would send their trades to Joe, and he would ensure that the trades were done. Very quickly, however, Joe started to make his own suggestions on trading strategy and in 1995 Joe's ideas were behind some of the most profitable trades for the year. Joe quickly established himself as a generator of original and distinctive investment strategies. His role of executing other managers' trades came to an end.

By 1998, Joe was running the macro-economic research group for Moore Capital and was responsible for covering the economic prospects for the major G10 economies. Over the years, Joe has been responsible for a number of very distinct and profitable trading ideas. He has a unique ability to distance himself from the muddle of consensus thinking and is prepared to think through an economic situation to its potential conclusions, even if such conclusions take years to unravel. His time horizon and ability to stand apart from conventional thinking mark him out, as does his ability to take complex economic issues and simplify them to a rational conclusion.

Joe's thinking on the current economic problems has been well chronicled within Moore Capital. Many analysts have subsequently claimed that they not only saw the credit crisis coming but understood exactly why it would unfold in the way it did. Joe genuinely did see the crisis coming and his rationale for its causes and its effects were laid out clearly well before the crisis became a crisis. In this sense, his thinking on how the economic situation will evolve over the coming decade needs close scrutiny. There are many factors that, as investors, need our specific attention. From an investment perspective, the economic environment has rarely been as difficult as it is right now. Governments face the tremendous challenge of re-gaining confidence. Fiscal policy has become a race between the ability to generate economic growth and investors patience in government credibility. How will this race resolve? Roseman explores this conundrum in full detail. It is not so much that he thinks outside the box as that he genuinely has no interest in where the box is to start with. The idea that a unique confluence of economic fault lines are coming together at the same time to create a form of "Economic Cascadia" is one that should make this book a must-read for anyone interested in the economic outlook, investments, society at large and capitalism in general.

Preface

About a decade ago, the husband of one of my wife's friends called me one evening. He had heard from his wife that I was "in financial markets" and that I worked at one of the big hedge funds.

I had never spoken to the guy before, but he was clearly on a mission. He told me that he had inherited some money and he wanted to invest it. He went on to tell me that he had another friend "in the markets" who had a fantastic penthouse, drove a flashy car and was loaded.

His friend, I was told, knew "the secret". He explained that I also knew "the secret" and he wanted to know it too. He assured me that he knew it was a closely guarded secret, but nonetheless, based on the fact that his wife was my wife's friend, he felt I could stretch the normal rules and let an outsider in on "the secret". At this point, I was a little confused.

I asked him exactly what he meant. So he spelt it out for me. "The secret", he explained, is how to turn small amounts of money into a fortune by investing in the right shares. "Oh, that secret", I replied.

I asked him how much he had to invest, what time horizon he was thinking of, what size of fortune he had in mind and how much risk he was willing to take. Well, it turned out that he had £2000 to invest, and he wanted to see it grow into £8000 within 3 months and was not really happy to be exposed to anything too risky. He certainly wouldn't consider anything that might lose him the £2000.

I gave him the best advice I could, that it was impossible to replicate his preferred outcome without taking enormous risks. I suggested going to a casino, placing the money on red and if he won to leave it on red for the next spin. He asked why I had chosen red and not black. Uhm.

I explained that this way he would have around a 25% probability of achieving his outcome in just one quick evening. But that was about as good as I could offer. He ended the conversation by stating that he realised that I, just like his friend, was not prepared to disclose "the secret". He was not happy.

Despite popular belief, it is most often the case that success is not about luck or being "in the know". Rather, it comes about (as Harry Hartman once said) when preparation meets opportunity. This book is about preparing for an economic future that could be unlike anything any living investor has experienced. In the 2007/8 period, a hedge fund manager named John Paulson became one of the richest men in the world. In one year he amassed a fortune of some $3.5bn by anticipating the US sub-prime crisis. Making that money wasn't about luck. Paulson spent a stunning amount of time in the year or two before the crisis unfolded investigating and understanding what was happening, doing research into the depth of the impending problem and then examining how to utilise the situation to generate enormous profits for himself and his investors. Paulson then waited for the right opportunity to present itself, and he was most definitely prepared when it did.

This book is not a get-rich-quick scheme. Nor, thankfully, is it a get-poor-quick scheme either, as so many books touting fortune-making opportunities appear to be. This book is about capital preservation. The coming economic environment is going to be more treacherous than anything since the 1930s. This book aims to provide alternatives to the standard thinking on economics and investment.

Between 1980 and 2000, just about everything that could go right for equity investors went right. Since 2000, just about everything that could go wrong has gone wrong. This book aims to explain why the economic environment of the last decade has treated equity investors so badly and why the coming decades might see that continue. It also aims to explain what type of assets will provide profitable returns for investors and what type of economic environment we are likely to experience.

The term "financial repression" was first coined by Stanford University economists, Shaw and McKinnon in 1973. Academic research by Professor Reinhart in 2011 described the world we are entering as one of financial repression. She argues that governments typically adopt such a policy when they are faced with overbearing debt burdens.

To the man on the street, what does "financial repression" really mean? The long and short of it is that returns from savings are consistently lower than inflation. Invest your hard-earned savings at 2% per annum and see inflation rise by 4% per annum. In other words, the government is facilitating the process of taking from savers to bail out those who had borrowed too much. In the current situation, most western governments have borrowed way too much. It is not hard to see why governments may indulge in the process of financial repression.

But the real problem that investors will confront over the coming 10-20 years is being faced with an economic environment that has no comparable precedent. Most economists use mathematical equations that rely on mean-reversion as an implicit part of their forecasting outlook. These econometric equations work well when the future looks like the past, but when new and totally different factors come into play, economists using econometrics become irrelevant and misleading.

My former boss at Moore Capital once heard someone state in a meeting that the market was always right. His response was that the market was always wrong, but we never knew for sure by how much and in what direction. If that is true, and it seems so blatantly so, then investors need to be particularly wary when faced with a radically different set of factors influencing economic growth and markets. The coming 10-20 years will see exactly that. The investment markets of the world will be faced with an entire cocktail of new and essentially unique economic fault lines with which to contend. On their own, each fault line would represent a major concern, but when taken together they represent what will likely be seen in the future as an inflection point for financial markets – an Economic Cascadia. No investment philosophy should be set in stone and get-rich-quick panaceas do not exist. Being prepared for the economic outlook puts an investor considerably ahead of the crowd.

So, I am left with an obvious unanswered question. Is there a secret? In truth, the secret has been out in the open for a very long period of time. As Edgar Allan Poe stated (The Purloined Letter 1844), "The best place to hide anything is in plain view." In this book, where do you look?

SWAG is an acronym for Silver, Wine, Art and Gold. I first put together the acronym for an article I wrote for the financial magazine "Investment Week". SWAG represents an asset class with specific investment characteristics. This book is about why SWAG assets should now form a part of any portfolio and why the coming economic horizon may make such assets even more important.

For those who want to understand the economic background to how we arrived at the current impasse, read Chapters 1-5. For those interested in the nitty-gritty of how quantitative easing and money printing affect the investment horizon and the rationale behind

SWAG investments, add chapters 6-7. For those who really only want to look at the assets I have selected and their characteristics, these are detailed in full from Chapter 8 through to 14. And if interest is specifically in one component of SWAG, say wine, then the Chapter to head to is within this range. Chapters 15-16 look at how some of the major secular trends of the future are unfolding and how this will affect SWAG assets. Chapter 17 explores how SWAG assets would fare under differing economic conditions. Chapters 18 and 19 are "how to" chapters, looking at some of the more practical issues of allocating money to SWAG and the accompanying need for robustness in a portfolio. Understanding the economic and monetary rationale for investing in SWAG assets is an important element of this book. But it is not essential. If you want to dive straight into the heart of the assets, do. Each chapter has a short summary at the end, so if you want to spend less than 15 minutes getting an idea of the book, just read the summaries.

Acknowledgments

This book has been written "in my head" for a very long time. It forms the essence of how I look at economics and investments. To those that say I am talking my own book, then quite literally I can now agree. But this would have stayed in my head had it not been for the encouragement and prompting of my friend and former colleague, Marc Cheval. For at least a decade, Marc and I have bounced ideas around and examined and stretched thinking about the very issues discussed in this book. Marc, thank you for pushing me into writing this book. It would most definitely not have happened without your encouragement.

I would also like to thank my wife, Caroline, for her patience in dealing with me whilst writing this book. And also for correcting my many sentences that begin with the word "And". Caroline, I know just how many times you re-read the manuscript. Thank you for all the errors and problems that you found. And thank you for all the time and patience you have devoted. Thank you also for giving encouragement when I was flagging.

I would also like to thank Lawrence Gosling for giving me the opportunity to write for "Investment Week" and for his total support for this book. Lawrence, many thanks.

Ian Amstad has been a friend for a very long time. Thank you, Ian, for taking the time to proofread the book and also for making an enormous contribution to the section on wine. Those that can detect a higher quality of writing and grammar in the wine section will recognise Ian's input.

Finally, I would like to thank my former employers, Louis Bacon and Elaine Crocker. I spent some 16 years at Moore Capital working for Louis and Elaine, and I can say honestly that I would not change a single day of it. There is no question that Moore Capital allowed me the mental freedom to work in a way that has allowed me to develop in the way I have. For that career of unfettered freedom, thank you.

CHAPTER 1

1980-2000: Cult of the Equity

How did we become so addicted to equities?

"Equities always go up. Never be short equities if you want a career in finance". This was the advice given to me in 1994 by one of my Moore Capital mentors early in my career. At the height of the internet bubble in 1999, he reminded me of his former advice. He had been spot on. However, as the internet bubble was reaching its climax, my mentor started to get worried about equities for the first time in his professional career.

The 20 year period following the Paul Volcker *revolution* at the turn of the 1980s saw an almost perfect confluence of events for equity markets. Volcker was the head of the US Federal reserve who decided that inflation had to be conquered. From that moment onwards (seemingly), just about everything that could go right for equities went right. If one had invested in the US equity market in the late 1970s and held that investment for the subsequent twenty years, then according to the Barclays Capital Equity Gilt study, that investor would have seen a return on investment of 12.8% per annum in real terms (i.e. even after taking account of inflation). The returns on the UK equity market were about the same.

To put this into some context, I have created a hypothetical investor who throughout much of the last century decides to invest money in the US equity market. On each occasion that he invests money, he holds that investment for the subsequent twenty year period. The investor decides to make investments every five years and he starts making those investments back in 1929. What sort of returns would he have seen over time? For the purposes of *this* study, all the returns are in real terms so the effects of inflation are removed.

Date of initial investment	Real return on US equities if held for next 20 years (% p.a.)	Real value of $1000 if held for next 20 years
1929	2.9	$1771
1934	9.3	$5921
1939	10.1	$6851
1944	11.6	$8980
1949	11.0	$8062
1954	3.1	$1842
1959	2.4	$1607
1964	2.1	$1515
1969	5.0	$2653
1974	9.3	$5921
1979	12.8	$11122
1984	9.7	$6970
1989	5.8	$3088

So, if an investor had placed his money for investment in December 1959, 20 years later he would have seen a real return averaging 2.4% p.a., turning $1000 into $1607. However, as can be seen from the table above, the 20 year period from 1979 was as good a moment to invest in equities as any time in history. $1000 invested in 1979, growing at 12.8% p.a., turned into over $11,000 twenty years later. The late 1970s clearly promised a great deal for those that could see the potential. But what exactly was it about the 1980s and 1990s that made equity investments so attractive?

In the late 1970s, Volcker's sledgehammer approach to attacking inflation saw bond yields start the period at a generational high. For the next 20 years, as central banks seemingly took control of inflation moderation, bond yields dropped consistently, underpinning a long-term re-rating for equity valuations. Labour markets were de-unionised and with the assistance of massive technological advances became substantially more flexible. Global outsourcing provided an almost unending supply of effective and cheap global labour. Unemployment fell without generating wage inflation. Productivity saw a huge fillip. Demographics were supportive. The end of the Cold War provided the so-called peace dividend. Having spiked to $40 per barrel at the time of the Iraq-Iran war in the late 70s, oil prices eased throughout the 1980s, and typically traded in a $10-20 range through the 1990s. Oil was cheap and so too were most raw materials. Thanks to the fact that financial markets had not been deregulated, household borrowing started the 1980s at a very low level. There was tremendous room for households to raise their borrowing. Households didn't disappoint. The economic boom saw government budgets improve. The government gross financial debt as a percentage of GDP was lower in the US and UK in 2000 than it had been 20 years earlier. This was a golden era for equity investors.

The above-list of tailwinds is by no means exhaustive. But, just about everything that could go right, did. And equities flew. I once remember a very successful equity trader berate me for questioning the value of the equity market. I was foolish for trying to evaluate "value" because, I was told, "Equities just go up. Why try to fight nature?"

However, having spent twenty years in an almost perfect equity environment, equity investors (and analysts) became normed into expecting the good times to roll forever. The buy-the-dip mentality that had worked so well for two decades was now firmly entrenched in the equity investors' psyche. However, perhaps more worrying was the fact that equity investors now tied this belief system that had been embedded into them after two decades into confidence in central bank policy. The belief system was based on the expectation that equities had always (well at least for the previous twenty years) provided excellent returns and that, importantly, policy-makers would always make the right choices to underpin the equity markets. This belief system became encapsulated in the term – the "Greenspan Put." The "Greenspan Put" is quoted on Wikipedia, which neatly describes it as one where:

> The Fed's pattern of providing ample liquidity resulted in the investor perception of put protection on asset prices. Investors increasingly believed that in a crisis or downturn, the Fed would step in and inject liquidity until the problem got better. Invariably, the Fed did so each time, and the perception became firmly embedded in asset pricing in the form of higher valuation, narrower credit spreads, and excess risk taking.

Stated simply, the theory was that one just needed to own equities to become rich. If anything happened in the economy that threatened the equity market, one could simply rely on the policy-makers to do whatever monetary manipulation was necessary to remedy any untoward dips along the way. The belief system became so powerful that it almost certainly became a part of creating the economic catastrophe that subsequently unfolded. Investors became convinced that losing wasn't a possibility. Investors became convinced that central banks could always be relied upon to keep asset markets healthy. This reliance created a paradox, and the subsequent upheaval in both the markets and real economy can, at least partially be explained by what has come to be known as the Stockdale Paradox.

The Stockdale Paradox

In 1965, Admiral James Stockdale was shot down during a mission over Vietnam and was imprisoned in what was known as the "Hanoi Hilton" for the next eight years. Despite repeated torture, no prisoner's rights and absolutely no certainty of survival, Stockdale did everything he could to ensure the (mental and physical) survival of other prisoners as well as himself. He put together rules for how other prisoners could deal with torture and other mistreatment. He also continued an ongoing "war" against his captors. He once injured himself with a chair and a razor in order to prevent his captors taking videotape recordings of him as a "well-treated" prisoner. Stockdale's remarkable story is detailed in an interview in Jim Collins book "Good to Great".

In that interview, Collins asked Stockdale what factors distinguished those that survived the ordeal and those that did not. Stockdale's answer created what is now known as the Stockdale Paradox. Although Stockdale had tremendous faith in his ability to survive, it was not blind faith. Stockdale noted that it was always the most optimistic of prisoners who failed to make it out alive. To quote Stockdale directly, "They were the ones who said, 'We're going to be out by Christmas.' And Christmas would come, and Christmas would go. Then they'd say, 'We're going to be out by Easter.' And Easter would come, and Easter would go. And then Thanksgiving, and then it would be Christmas again. And they died of a broken heart."

Blind faith in this situation prevented some prisoners from confronting the harsh reality of their situation. Such self-delusion may provide some crutch of comfort, but it will only ever be a short-term fix. As Stockdale put it, "you must never confuse faith that you will prevail in the end with the discipline to confront the most brutal of facts of your current reality, whatever they might be."

So, for the twenty years up to 2000, equity investors had the heady mixture of both an almost perfect macro-economic environment and a "Greenspan Put" that essentially promised them that monetary policy would be used to stimulate economic activity should the merest need be seen. The result was the birth and maturity of the cult of the equity. Equity investors became so normed by the process that investment thought started to be replaced with blind faith. And as the twenty year process unfolded, blind faith became more and more prevalent amongst equity thinking. The Dot.Com bust in 2000 provides so many case studies of such blind faith as to beggar belief. Companies no longer needed a track record of making money. The "E" of the Price Earnings ratio was not necessary. All that was needed was "faith" and the promise of sales.

In my opinion, we are now some ten years past the bursting of that equity bubble. The cult of the equity has been dead for a decade. Yet, the Stockdale Paradox still prevails for so many. So many investors still cling on, using little more than blind faith, hoping that the good times for equity investors are just around the corner. The "Greenspan Put" bred into investors an almost Pavlovian response to buy dips. But for a decade now, such strategies have not worked. Yet still the Stockdale Paradox prevails. The time to buy equities will come. But, as Stockdale would argue, it will do so only once investors "confront the most brutal of facts of their current reality, whatever they might be." We may still be some time away from that happening. For, just as the 1980-2000 era was one where just about everything went right for equities, the 2000-2010 era has been one where just about everything has gone wrong. The key issue going forward will be to evaluate realistically how much more could go wrong, and how long that might take to heal.

Chapter 1 Summary

- Between 1980 and 2000, just about everything that could go right for the equity investor went right. Inflation moved onto a gradually declining path. Labour markets were deregulated and outsourcing provided cheap global labour. Demographics were supportive. Oil prices were relatively cheap. Household and government borrowing were generally low. The Cold War ended giving the so-called peace dividend.

- Investors saw stunning returns from equity investment over this period. The cult of the equity was born and buy-the-dip mentality became a legitimised investment technique.

- Investor faith in central bank policy rose to an all-time high.

- In fact, investors became so enamoured with equities as an asset class that a form of "Stockdale Paradox" developed. Investors developed almost blind faith in the ability of the central banks despite mounting evidence to suggest that the economic environment was deteriorating.

- Since 2000 or so, just about everything that could go wrong for equities has gone wrong. Returns over the decade have been amongst the lowest on record. And still investors seem addicted to equity investment. The Stockdale Paradox persists. As Stockdale himself observed, eventually it is those who cling on unrealistically to a hope that eventually die of a broken heart.

CHAPTER 2

Where did it All Go Wrong: the last 10 years

So, as previously argued, the Stockdale Paradox provides a partial explanation for why the current situation has developed. However, it is only a partial explanation. A reluctance to confront the harsh realities of the problem has most definitely enhanced the scale of the current problem. Basically, central bankers, politicians and investors stuck their respective heads in the sand. But, an understanding of how the "Greenspan Put" gradually hypnotised investors is also necessary. By understanding how the disease took hold, one can at least begin to formulate a cure.

It is not clear when, exactly, it happened, but over the course of Greenspan's tenure as head of the US Federal Reserve (1987-2006), the idea that interest rate policy was a tool to finesse (or even eradicate) the business cycle became more and more commonly accepted. At the merest hint of weaker growth, monetary policy was eased. This created an entirely new type of cycle: Weakening economy. Lower interest rates. Higher gearing. Recovery. Weakening economy. Even lower interest rates. Even higher gearing. And so on. Households were encouraged to borrow and the mentality of spending today what one *might* earn tomorrow became commonplace. Such a policy, of course, has tremendous appeal to consumers. Borrowing becomes the equivalent of an addictive drug. The more one takes, the more one needs until all rational thought process is removed. In many senses, excess levels of borrowing act very much like heroin and can be just as destructive.

Central banks believed they would always be able to re-stimulate an economy should it prove necessary. This was the game-plan for G10 central banks. And it created a very specific outcome where household borrowing escalated until it became so high that the sheer weight of it almost certainly precipitated a recession – the 2008 credit crunch. Of course, the "greedy" bankers were also to blame for making credit too easily available to those that could not afford it.

But, blame must also be placed on the "greedy" consumers who wanted to buy today what they couldn't afford today but *might* be able to afford tomorrow. There is a classic bestseller entitled "The Richest Man in Babylon". The narrative follows two poor men as they attempt to gain wisdom from a former friend who had become very wealthy. The book contains a list of axioms which purportedly lead to wealth creation. These axioms, when put together, form a fool-proof formula for becoming rich. Yet, whenever anyone reads the book, the result generally is a feeling of being cheated. The essence of the formula is simple. To become rich, one needs simply to spend less than one earns on a consistent basis.

But this was certainly not the mentality that prevailed in the years running up to the credit crisis in 2008. In fact, central banks almost encouraged consumers to do the opposite. The size of the consumer sector within the advanced economies generally became larger and larger. Governments, as testified by the fact that they rarely if ever run budget surpluses, also lived by the rule of spending more than they earn. Becoming rich by constantly spending less than one earns is a blatant truism. What happens when consumers and governments do the exact opposite? Well, logic would suggest it is a fool-proof formula for becoming poor.

Indeed. The scale of indebtedness that has occurred over the last 10-15 years (not just amongst households but also governments) has become so substantial that monetary policy has almost become neutered. To a bankrupt man, whether he is paying 5% on his loans or 10% is irrelevant. He cannot afford to repay anything. As a result, monetary policy in the G10 has effectively become inoperable and alternative measures, shock measures, like quantitative easing are now needed. At some point, somebody needs to ask the question why monetary policy has become impotent. Wouldn't it be reasonable to assume that with interest rate policy having been at generational lows for several years and with government budgets at generational highs, one might have expected reasonable economic growth? But economic growth just hasn't materialised. Instead, unemployment has risen. The economic engine appears broken. Who to blame?

It is harsh to lay the blame at just the central bankers. Economists as a breed seem to have been taken in by the same mirage. Many economies have over-borrowed. Many have seen a huge amount of poor investment and business growth in areas that are simply unsustainable. Where is the policy error in allowing bad investments to fail? This is how successful economies have operated for centuries. It is economic Darwinism. Yet, throughout the 1990s and into much of the last decade, the merest sign of economic weakness was seized upon by economists who would then put pressure on central banks to *"rescue"* the situation by (once again) easing monetary policy. What economists appear to have forgotten is that recessions are a necessary evil in the healthy forward progress of an economy. Survival of the fittest has a purpose.

Indeed, in many circumstances, recessions are good. Now, I appreciate that this may arouse a lot of negative response. But, I will say it again. Recessions are usually good. They remove unviable businesses and allow capital to relocate to businesses that do deserve a role. Unemployment results in re-training and also redeployment into more productive areas of the economy. It isn't a pleasant process but it is one that allows an economy to remain healthy. But recessions don't win elections, and politicians are drawn instead to economic advice that promotes borrow-and-spend policies, and measures that try to avoid any economic pain. It is the economic equivalent of King Cnut. What is needed is cold turkey.

Think of it like this; when a person goes to the doctor for a check-up and the doctor says that they need to lose weight and get fit or run the risk of a heart attack, that person may then sensibly decide to join a gym. Is the gym good or bad? I am not saying it is pleasant, but it is not bad. Recessions are like economic health kicks. They are not pleasant but they are necessary and typically they leave an economy healthier. Of course, it will always be easier and more enjoyable to sit back, drink some beer and eat some more cheese-coated nachos. However, thanks in part to misguided central bank policy, gearing grew out of control and G10 economies became fat and lazy, preferring to spend future earning and incur debt rather than raising productivity by being efficient. So convinced were central banks with their mastery of the business cycle that households became addicted to borrowing and addicted to their perceived increase in wealth and spending power. But it was an illusion of well-being.

In an attempt to eradicate the business cycle, central banks, then, created a new type of business cycle of ever-lower policy rates and ever-higher gearing. Gearing has now risen to a point where in some countries, despite policy rates being at virtually zero, the risk of higher rates sends fears of a renewed recession. Japan's public debt levels are now so high that policy rates much above zero would send the interest costs alone into the stratosphere. Japan is not alone. As each successive crisis has unfolded since 2000, policy rates around the developed world have <u>needed</u> to go lower and lower until even zero interest rates have not been enough.

Thus, we have arrived at a point in economic history where unconventional monetary policy in the shape of quantitative easing is no longer so unconventional.

Indeed, as of February 2012, the Bank of England embarked on yet another round of quantitative easing arguing that the preceding weakness of economic activity threatened to create a deflationary environment. So, now that interest rates cannot be lowered any more, central banks have been pushed into a corner and are forced to resort to outright money printing. This process has been implemented across the major economies. It is worth categorising quantitative easing for what it really is. Investopedia provides a perfectly good explanation of quantitative easing:

What Does Quantitative Easing Mean?

A government monetary policy occasionally used to increase the money supply by buying government securities or other securities from the market. Quantitative easing increases the money supply by flooding financial institutions with capital, in an effort to promote increased lending and liquidity.

Central banks tend to use quantitative easing when interest rates have already been lowered to near 0% levels and have failed to produce the desired effect. The major risk of quantitative easing is that, although more money is floating around, there is still a fixed amount of goods for sale. This will eventually lead to higher prices or inflation.

Quantitative easing is the public sector's version of a Ponzi scheme. The illusion of wealth being created through quantitative easing is the same illusion as wealth created by the "returns" of a Ponzi scheme.

> A **Ponzi scheme** is a fraudulent investment that pays returns to investors from their own money or (more usually) the money paid by subsequent investors. The scheme purports to have an underlying (and valid) business that generates genuine profits. There is no genuine underlying business. The Ponzi scheme usually entices new investors by offering attractive returns. However, for those returns to persist, an ever-increasing number of new investors are required. It is this new money that is subsequently paid out to earlier investors as "profits" that gives the scheme the appearance of credibility.
>
> The system is destined to collapse because the "profits" that are distributed eventually overtake the scheme's ability to attract new investors. The fraud is named after Charles Ponzi, who used the technique in the 1920s.

This poses a very difficult question to an investor. In a world beset with the risk of sovereign defaults courtesy of exploding government debt, with wide-scale use of money printing and with economic growth seemingly unable to hit trend, resulting in high and rising levels of unemployment, the investment backdrop for an investor is stunningly difficult. The key question an investor must ask is how to preserve capital.

Typically, markets go through three climate phases. The <u>sunny</u> outlook is the sweet spot where the backdrop is generally positive for equity investment. In such an environment, it is generally quite hard to lose money by owning equities. Then there are the <u>cloudy</u> periods, characterised by much higher uncertainty where risks are generally balanced and sector performance and asset allocation become crucial. Some boats are floated and some are sunk. Then there are economic episodes that can only be described as <u>stormy</u>, when risk of capital loss for most asset classes is so high that investors only need address one issue: capital preservation.

When in a sweet spot, anyone can make money. When one moves away from sweet spots, it is always important to know where to invest and importantly where to hide. In today's environment, fixed income no longer provides that hiding place. Owning cash in a world of quantitative easing could be destructive. The lack of economic growth poses a real threat to Sovereign credit ratings, and sovereign default hangs like the sword of Damocles over equity markets. There is no question that we are in an investment world where capital preservation is of paramount importance, yet at the same time all the traditional safe havens have become embedded with new and untoward risks.

Chapter 2 summary

- Through the 1980s, 1990s and the first decade of the new millennium, central banks in the major economies increasingly came to believe that they could control the business cycle. Investors believed them. The "Greenspan Put" was born. Investors believed that central banks could revive economies whenever it looked even vaguely like an economy was starting to weaken.

- Central banks (and investors) forgot that recessions are the economic equivalent of going to the gym. Recessions cleanse an economy of unprofitable, unviable and unproductive businesses and create the potential for new more efficient businesses to take their place. Recessions eventually lead to a healthier economy.

- Yet, whenever economic weakness materialised, central banks stimulated monetary policy by cutting interest rates. This created a new type of business cycle of ever-lower policy rates and ever-higher gearing. As each successive crisis unfolded since 2000, policy rates around the developed world have needed to go lower and lower until even zero interest rates have not been enough to generate trend GDP growth. Governments and central banks then turned to *unconventional* monetary policy in the shape of Quantitative Easing.

- Yet, to be unconventional, it implies that its usage must be rare. Regrettably, the use of Quantitative Easing since 2009 has become increasingly more common as economic growth has failed to respond as traditional thinking suggests it should have.

- This poses a very difficult question to an investor. In a world beset with the risk of sovereign defaults courtesy of exploding government debt, with wide-scale use of money printing and with economic growth seemingly unable to hit trend, resulting in high levels of unemployment, the investment backdrop for an investor is stunningly difficult. The key question an investor must ask is how to preserve capital.

CHAPTER 3

The Coming Decade and the Risks to be Faced

Many economists spend their time using highly complex econometric equations in order to predict the economy in 1-2 years' time. In my opinion, it is a total waste of time. If one goes back 15 years and looks at the consensus of economic opinion for what GDP growth will be in 1 to 2 years' time, it ALWAYS says the same thing – trend growth. Economists basically have no idea where GDP growth will be in 1-2 years' time. The use of complex equations is only there to camouflage the fact that there is little substance to their economic forecast. And since central bank policy acts with a 1-2 year lag, this means that policy-makers are pretty much always acting in the dark. Any advice they receive from economists using complex econometric equations should be instantly dismissed. It is worthless.

So, when one sees the economic consensus predicting that GDP growth is set to recover, take it with a pinch of salt. Investing in equities based on such reasoning is likely to produce the same dire performance of the last decade. It is partly an element of the Stockdale Paradox where blind optimistic faith drives the forecast and partly a reliance on econometrics which have at their heart the driving force of mean reversion. It is human nature to like mean reversion. In reality, mean reversion should exist mainly in the scientific laboratory since in real life, particularly in an investment world, it is a recipe for disaster. Many people are still waiting for the price of Enron to mean-revert back to its old levels. But, mean reversion is a powerful human "need", and economists and market participants still keep anticipating a normal recovery. Eventually, the Stockdale Paradox will prevail. Eventually the "hope" that is inherent in mean reversion will give way to a more realistic view of the coming period.

There is another good reason why economists keep over-predicting economic growth. In a recent paper by Professors Reinhart and Rogoff, it was argued that once the accumulation of debt exceeds a certain level, economic growth becomes weighed down and incapable of being anything other than limp and sub-potential (more on this in Chapter 5). In recent years, the evidence seems to support their hypothesis. Despite record-low levels of interest rates and copious amounts of quantitative easing, economic growth has been moribund. As one hedge fund manager I know once described it, the accelerator pedal is being floored, but the Ferrari is only hitting 45mph. Something is wrong with the engine. Reinhart and Rogoff may have hit on one of the key reasons.

Well, one of them anyway. In fact there are many things wrong. But, at the risk of over-simplification, the current crisis has now morphed into one of debt default risk.

Public sector deficits across the G10 have reached such alarmingly high levels that the risk of an imminent new recession would create an impossible debt dynamic for most economies. Weak growth means bigger budget deficits. As the levels of debt rise, Rogoff and Reinhart would argue that in itself limits growth. A lack of growth means more unemployment, more government spending and less tax revenues, implying more budget deficits and more government debt and thus less economic growth. A vicious cycle emerges – a debt default dynamic.

Yes, we are in a potential debt default scenario. Politicians everywhere are looking for ways to "solve" the problem. There is a degree of surprise and shock as the crisis just doesn't seem to go away despite the scale of stimulus applied.

Looked at in simplistic terms, the numerator in the equation (level of debt) is growing faster than the denominator (nominal GDP). Hence the debt/GDP ratio is growing. In the US, 10 years ago the ratio stood at 54%. In 2012 it will almost certainly reach over 100% of GDP. In the UK, it stood at 40% ten years ago. In 2012 it will approach 100% too. Rogoff and Reinhart suggested that, historically, a debt ratio of over 90% caused a problem. The higher that debt ratio is, the bigger the problem.

Policy-makers have a limited number of options. They can try to raise taxes and cut spending so that the debt accumulation is cut back. As both US and UK politicians will attest, this arouses an enormous amount of idealistic friction between those who believe that tightening fiscal policy in the midst of a potential recession is counter-productive and those that believe fiscal prudence is, at all times, needed.

The alternative policy option is to focus on boosting the denominator, nominal GDP. If nominal GDP can be boosted enough, then the debt/GDP ratio will fall. Nominal GDP is composed of two components. The first is real GDP which represents actual economic growth. The second component is inflation. So when real GDP growth is added to inflation, the result is called nominal GDP. Those that advocate boosting nominal GDP by expanding the money supply do so not really knowing how much of the growth will come from real GDP and how much from inflation. For the purposes of avoiding default, it doesn't really matter to them. But, from an investors' perspective it is crucial to make the differentiation.

Which policy choice will work? Fiscal rectitude would, once upon a time, have been the correct solution. However, events have escalated somewhat. Despite the fact that interest rates have collapsed to essentially zero, US and UK net interest payments on their rapidly expanding mountain of debt have now risen to between 2-3% of GDP. So, even if both countries ran a balanced budget on all other areas, they would still need to borrow between 2-3% of GDP each year just to pay their interest payments. The truth of the matter is that with budget deficits still wildly out of control and against a backdrop of GDP growth well below trend, the chance of the debt/GDP ratio stabilising in the next 5 years is very remote. Indeed, in 5 years' time maybe it is not unrealistic to imagine a debt/GDP ratio of 125% or more for G10 economies.

So investors find themselves in a position where GDP can't grow much because it is burdened by such a debt overhang. This is the Rogoff and Reinhart prognosis. Debt reduction is not possible now as the scale of cutbacks would just weaken economic growth further, leading to a cyclical rise in the budget deficit. Catch 22 for economics. It is no wonder that central banks are resorting to more and more printing of money via quantitative easing. Each time that they do, they roll the dice hoping to boost nominal GDP. And each time that printing money is involved, the risk of that nominal GDP boost being through inflation rather than real growth rises in probability. In reality, governments throughout history have found themselves in this situation many times. Typically, the outcome follows a fairly predictable pattern as governments impose what economists have come to call "financial repression."

Chapter 3 – Summary

- Economists who use history to try to predict the future will not see the bus that hits them. Economists, as a breed, know something is wrong, but still insist on using the same prediction toolkit that saw them fail to predict the crisis to start with.

- Despite enormous monetary and fiscal stimulus, the major OECD economies have not managed to generate adequate economic growth. The scale of the stimulus should have seen boom-time growth. But the economic engine seems broken. Hoping it will revive falls prey to the Stockdale Paradox. To understand why the engine is broken is key to being able to navigate an investment portfolio through the problem.

- Too much government debt may be one of the causes. Governments have been placed in a Catch 22 scenario. If they do not get control of the fiscal position (and the rising government debt levels), confidence will be lost and severe potential economic problems will arise. If they do try to impose fiscal austerity, this may just exacerbate the lack of prevailing economic weakness making the fiscal situation even worse.

- Governments have been in this spot before. Academic research shows that typically, the policy prescription that is adopted is one called "financial repression." Financial repression certainly provides a solution of a kind. But it brings with it all manner of unintended consequences.

CHAPTER 4

Financial Repression

The term "financial repression" was first introduced into everyday economic terminology by Stanford University economists Shaw and McKinnon. The economic definition is complex. According to a research paper by Giovannini and Melo for the American Economic Review in 1993:

> Financial repression is a combination of controls on international capital flows with restrictions on domestic interest rates. The result is an artificially low cost of domestic funding to governments.

Given the explosion in debt during the last 20 years, more and more academic research has examined financial repression. According to a 2011 NBER Working Paper (16893) by Reinhart and Sbrancia entitled "The Liquidation of Government Debt":

> Historically, periods of high indebtedness have been associated with a rising incidence of default or restructuring of public and private debts. A subtle

type of debt restructuring takes the form of "financial repression." Financial repression includes directed lending to government by captive domestic audiences (such as pension funds), explicit or implicit caps on interest rates, regulation of cross-border capital movements, and (generally) a tighter connection between government and banks. In the heavily regulated financial markets of the Bretton Woods system, several restrictions facilitated a sharp and rapid reduction in public debt/GDP ratios from the late 1940s to the 1970s. Low nominal interest rates help reduce debt servicing costs while a high incidence of negative real interest rates liquidates or erodes the real value of government debt. Thus, financial repression is most successful in liquidating debts when accompanied by a steady dose of inflation.

This is the more formal definition. Reinhart and Sbrancia, however, really cut to the point in the body of their report. This key point is also highlighted in the June 2011 paper by Reinhart, Kirkegaard and Sbrancia entitled "Financial Repression Redux". The key point is that financial repression is essentially a tax. The following is taken from the NBER Working Paper:

One of the main goals of financial repression is to keep nominal interest rates lower than would otherwise prevail. This effect, other things equal, reduces the governments' interest expenses for a given stock of debt and contributes to deficit reduction. However, when financial repression produces negative real interest rates, this also reduces or liquidates existing debts. It is a transfer from creditors (savers) to borrowers (in the historical episode under study here - the government).

The financial repression tax has some interesting political-economy properties. Unlike income, consumption, or sales taxes, the "repression" tax rate (or rates) are determined by financial regulations and inflation performance that are opaque to the highly politicized realm of fiscal measures. Given that deficit reduction usually involves highly unpopular expenditure reductions and (or) tax increases of one form or another, the relatively "stealthier" financial repression tax may be a more politically palatable alternative to authorities faced with the need to reduce outstanding debts.

Bottom line then is that interest rates are kept, artificially, below inflation rates. Academics need to be balanced about their analysis. I see myself as neither an academic nor an economist, so I can interpret the academic research as it appears. To me, the best definition of "financial repression" is that it is theft by those who have borrowed recklessly from those who have saved prudently. An example might be useful.

Imagine a person who has (over-)borrowed a significant amount to buy a big house. The person borrowed £250,000 to buy a £250,000 house and has a mortgage rate of 3%. He earns a salary of £20,000 per annum. He spends £2500 a year on food and £7500 a year on mortgage payments. In a period of financial repression, the government holds interest rates at this artificially low level for 10 years. Inflation, however, is allowed to rise to an average 5% per annum throughout the period. This 5% inflation applies to wage inflation, house inflation as well as food inflation. What will this person's balance sheet look like after a decade?

Well, in a decade, he will still owe £250,000 mortgage. His salary, however, will have risen to £32,577 per annum. His food bill will have risen too, to £4072 per annum. His mortgage costs will be the same. His house will have risen in value to £407,223. So, his net worth will have risen significantly. His mortgage costs will have shrunk from representing 37% of his salary at the start of the decade to just 23% by the end of the decade. The food costs still represent the same share of his income throughout the period. Financial repression has worked miracles for this over-borrowed individual.

However, now let's look at how it affects the prudent saver. Imagine a person who has saved throughout his lifetime in order to build a nest-egg for retirement. On the day of retirement, the nest-egg is worth £100,000 and it is invested in a government bond paying an interest rate of 2.5% per annum for 15 years. Let's also imagine that the cost of food shopping for the retiree is £2500 per annum. For the sake of simplicity, I will assume that there is no income tax to pay on his income. After a decade, the prudent saver will have seen his food costs rise to £4072 per annum. However, since he had retired he did not have the benefit of wage inflation. Instead, with interest rates being kept artificially low, his income remained static at £2500 per annum. This individual has seen his real cost of living decline sharply. Initially, his investment income covered his food costs. At the end of the decade of inflation, his investment income paid for his food from January through to around July, leaving him to draw on capital to pay for food for the remainder of the year.

These examples are meant to be highly simplified. However, from the examples it is very clear that in an environment where inflation is allowed to rise and where interest rates are kept artificially low, one type of person wins and one type of person loses. One section of society gets "taxed" by financial repression and another segment of society gets bailed out by that tax. The winners and losers are not hard to identify. The biggest winner is the largest and most reckless borrower – government. Yet, if financial repression represents the transfer of wealth away from those with savings to those who have over-borrowed, won't those with savings revolt against the process and kick-out the taxer when it comes to election time?

This poses an interesting issue. Who, exactly, is the biggest loser from financial repression? It is easy to see who wins; government, people who have large amounts of assets secured by borrowing, people with mortgages and jobs, investors in assets that benefit from rising inflation (and that includes banks). Government often try to argue that their policies are aimed at helping the more vulnerable in society. The win list suggests otherwise.

The reality is that in order for the "winners" to win, they need to be bailed out by the "losers". This is by no means an exhaustive list, but those being taxed by financial repression will include the retired who rely on a fixed income, those who are building a pension pot with high levels of fixed income in that pension, the prudent saver who believes that putting money aside in the building society for a rainy day, the person on low income who doesn't have a mortgage and those without jobs. In one way or another, this group of people will bail-out the borrowers.

Under normal circumstances, taxing the saver to bail-out the reckless borrower typically doesn't carry any particular risks to society. As academic research shows, it is a stealth tax that usually goes unnoticed as it takes place over an extended period of time and the source of the tax (government) is hard to see. It is the equivalent to the metaphorical frog in boiling water. Those being taxed are either unaware that they are being boiled or unable to see who is responsible for their increasing (financial) pain. Financial repression is a very devious tax. Yet, it is now in full use. Official interest rates in both the US and UK have been below headline inflation rates for a prolonged period of time. The Bank of England reduced base rates to 0.5% in March 2009 and as of February 2012, base rates have remained at 0.5%. Inflation as measured by CPI averaged 2.2% in 2009, 3.3% in 2010 and in 2011 averaged 4.5%. A similar picture is true for the US. Financial repression is here. Indeed, in the US, the Federal Reserve Bank has even stated that official interest rates will remain fixed for a prolonged period in the future. There is no question that financial repression is now a blatant policy objective.

However, there are a number of rare events taking place now that make the use of financial repression a very dangerous policy option. Indeed there is a toxic cocktail of factors that are occurring all at the same time that make the use of financial repression and the implicit money printing equivalent to opening an economic Pandora's Box. The following chapter takes a closer look at these factors.

Chapter 4 - Summary

- As the academics define it, one of the main goals of financial repression is to keep interest rates lower than would otherwise prevail. This effect tends to reduce the interest expense on a government's debt and contributes to budget deficit reduction.

- When financial repression produces negative real interest rates (i.e. interest rates lower than the level of inflation), this also reduces or liquidates existing debts. Academic study shows that throughout history, whenever governments have got themselves into a deep debt hole, financial repression has been one of the key policy actions that have bailed them out.

- Academics need to define their quarry very precisely. What does financial repression really mean? In short, it is a back-door strategy by government that in essence taxes those with savings (through inflation) in order to bail out those who have recklessly over-borrowed.

- Financial repression creates clear winners and clear losers. Someone needs to be bailed out. Someone needs to do the bailing. It is easy to see who wins; government, people who have large amounts of assets secured by borrowing, people with mortgages and jobs, investors in assets that benefit from rising inflation (and that includes banks). Government often try to argue that their policies are aimed at helping the more vulnerable in society. The win list suggests otherwise.

- And the losers? This is by no means an exhaustive list, but those being taxed by financial repression will include the retired who rely on a fixed income, those who are building a pension pot with high levels of fixed income in that pension, the prudent saver who believes that putting money aside in the building society for a rainy day, the person on low income who doesn't have a mortgage and those without jobs. In one way or another, this group of people will bail-out the borrowers.

- There are a number of rare events taking place now that make the use of financial repression a very dangerous policy option. Indeed there is a toxic cocktail of factors that are occurring all at the same time that make the use of financial repression and the implicit money printing equivalent to opening an economic Pandora's Box.

CHAPTER 5

The Economic Fault-lines;
Demography, Debt and Peak Supply

Demographics

For the first time (possibly ever), the demographic structure of the developed economies is set to become a major negative factor for growth. For the first time in UK history, people aged over 65 years outnumber children aged less than 5 years.

According to the World Bank, the proportion of UK dependents older than 65 years old relative to the working population (those aged 15-64) has risen from 17.5% in the early 1960s, to over 20% in the 1970s, to over 23% in the 1980s, to 28% currently. That 28% represents approximately 11.5 million people. One of the few things that can be predicted with reasonable confidence is future demographic trends. If one knows how many people there are in specific age groups, it is not rocket science to predict how many there will be in ten years' time. According to the UK pensions industry, the number of dependent pensioners by 2020 will have reached 13.5 million people. The rise of the pensioner class is happening across the industrialised world to varying degrees. In Japan the elderly dependency ratio has hit a staggering 38% already. In Germany it is currently 33%. At 22%, the US is in better shape, but is still rising rapidly.

Significant academic resources are applied to demographic expectations. Some analysts even argue that just about the only thing that is truly needed to make long-term economic projections are the dependency ratios. I wouldn't go that far, but I would go so far as to say that dependency ratios are a crucial and necessary part of the forecaster's toolkit.

Using the analysis of dependency ratios from the United Nations Department of Economic and Social Affairs, it is possible to display graphically the outlook for the dependency ratio for the coming decades. The following table shows what can reliably be expected.

Old-age dependency ratio*	1990	2010	2030	2050
US	19%	20%	33%	35%
UK	24%	25%	34%	40%
Japan	17%	35%	53%	70%
Germany	22%	31%	48%	57%
Italy	22%	31%	44%	62%
Greece	20%	28%	37%	55%
Developed economies	19%	24%	36%	45%
Emerging economies	7%	9%	15%	23%

*Number of people aged over 65yrs as proportion of working population

The United Nations database conveniently splits their analysis into developed countries against lesser developed areas too. This comparison is made in the last two rows of the table above.

As can be seen from the table, emerging economies start from a much healthier base. Over the last 20 years, there has been only a small rise in the age dependency ratio for emerging economies. For the more developed economies, the upward trend in age dependency has been more marked and from a higher level. What is really interesting, however, is what will happen over the coming decades. For the developed economies, the rise in the dependency ratio over the coming 20 years will be very substantial. If the demographics over the coming two decades are considered, the developed world appears to be at the cusp of a new era. This inflection point will bring with it a great deal of change and has to be considered when evaluating any economic expectation or indeed any investment expectation.

A study by the IMF in June 2011 by Howe and Jackson entitled "How Ready for Pensioners?" spells out the problem clearly. The study concludes that "global aging promises to affect every dimension of economic, social and political life." The study, however, is of particular interest as it aims to identify which economies are most prepared for the coming demographic shift. It covers 20 countries, including most of the major G10 economies as well as a selection of the larger emerging economies. The study creates two measures of preparedness. One measure ranks the 20 economies according to the projected burden of old-age dependency on the fiscal position of the economy. In other words it is a fiscal sustainability index. The second index ranks economies according to the projected standard of living implied by the existing pension and benefit system. Ideally, if a country scores highly on both measures, it is in a good position. The following tables depict the findings of the study.

Fiscal Sustainability Index		Income Adequacy Index	
Rank	Country	Rank	Country
1	India	1	Netherlands
2	Mexico	2	Brazil
3	Chile	3	United States
4	China	4	Germany
5	Russia	5	United Kingdom
6	Poland	6	Australia
7	Australia	7	Sweden
8	Japan	8	Chile
9	Canada	9	Spain
10	Sweden	10	India
11	United States	11	Canada
12	Korea	12	Japan
13	Switzerland	13	Poland
14	Germany	14	Switzerland
15	United Kingdom	15	Russia
16	Italy	16	France
17	France	17	Italy
18	Brazil	18	China
19	Netherlands	19	Korea
20	Spain	20	Mexico

A number of conclusions can be drawn from this study. The IMF, of course, needs to be politically correct. However, not even the IMF can avoid putting the boot into France and Italy, who respectively rank in the bottom quartile of both indices. To quote the study directly;

France and Italy spend so much on old age benefits and have so little fiscal room to accommodate future benefit growth that, even after reforms, they remain on a fiscally unsustainable course: both countries are moving towards retirement systems that are simultaneously inadequate and unaffordable.

There are other stark statistics that jump from this study. The countries that tend to be most fiscally prepared are, generally speaking, the emerging economies. The countries with the least fiscal room for manoeuvre are the G10 economies. As a general rule, and one highlighted by the study, the countries that are best prepared to meet the promises they have made to retirees are those countries that have promised them least. This suggests major problems for the G10 economies going forward.

Such problems are clear to see. Predicting this outcome is not rocket science. It is essentially inevitable. Back in 1986, The May Economic Outlook by the OECD contained an interesting analysis by Chouraqui, Jones and Montador entitled "Public Debt in a Medium-Term Perspective." The study anticipated explicitly the risk to public finances from ageing demographics. It stated that:

If the stance of fiscal policies and the levels of real interest rates projected for 1986 remained the same in the future, and assuming that output grew at its potential rate from 1986 projected levels, the debt ratios would rise rapidly in most OECD countries.......recognition of (future) social security or pension liabilities - which are not usually taken into account in the definition of gross or net debt - would tend to increase projected government deficits relative to output as the population ages and as social security plans mature, unless policy is changed to raise taxes or to reduce benefits. Considering this factor substantially changes the outlook for debt ratios in a number of countries. In particular, debt ratios in Japan and Germany, instead of declining, would at first stabilize and then, after ten years, begin to rise rapidly.

So, back in 1986 the OECD saw the impending debt problem. They were right. Yet, their vision and advice was ignored by most OECD governments. Denial is a human trait. If the outlook for the future is grim, it is so often human nature to ignore it and hope it will go away. This is particularly true for politicians where doing the right thing for the economy conflicts directly with their respective opinion poll popularity. Spending cuts and fiscal austerity do not win votes. Back in 1986, the OECD was suggesting that in the absence of such fiscal repair, the debt problem would just get bigger. How did the OECD governments respond? They did the exact opposite. Faced with a debt hole and an impending demographic deterioration, they decided to dig a deeper debt hole. History will look back at this economic era and sensible people will ask: "What on earth were governments thinking?" The difference between the OECD forecast in 1986 and the current position is that whereas back in 1986 there was fiscal scope for governments to act sensibly, today there is no room. The deterioration in demographics will become increasingly more pronounced and this demographic inflection will bring considerable change.

What sort of change will this inflection point bring? For a start, the retiring population will shift from being taxpayers to being receivers of state retirement benefits. The government will receive less in the way of income tax revenues and will have to pay out more in the way of pension benefits. Further, for any individual, the vast majority of the money that they are likely to need to be spent on health issues occurs during their older years. A 1987 study by the National Research Council entitled "Demographic Change and the Well-Being of Children and the Elderly" reported that almost one-third of health care expenditure is devoted to the 11% of the population aged over 65 years. A number of academic studies have shown that health care expenditure rises increasingly with age.

A number of studies have underlined the observation that this relationship is mainly the result of the concentration of health spending in the period just before death (Lubitz and Riley 1993; McGrail et al 2000; Himsworth et al 1999, Zweifel et al 1999). However, it is an observable fact that as age increases the amount of money spent on healthcare rises. It makes sense that as an individual grows older, their probability of dying rises. If most health spending occurs just before death, then that is indeed likely to happen to an elderly person. The bottom line, however, is that as the elderly grow in number, so too will the pressures on governments to allocate more government spending to the healthcare for those elderly. An ageing demographic really isn't helpful for a government's fiscal plans. Given that most G10 governments start the decade with record budget deficits and high and rising debt/GDP ratios, the onset of a demographic inflection point could not have been more ill-timed.

Another key change will be that the retirees will see their income change in format. The retiree income stream will shift from wages (when employed) to investment income and pension (when retired). That retirement income will likely come from two areas; first, from privately invested savings and second, from the state and corporate pension schemes. All these sources will be heavily invested in fixed income assets.

And herein lies the rub. The biggest growing segment of society amongst the developed industrialised economies is the elderly. This segment represented 19% of the working population in 1990. Today it represents 24% and this share will rise inexorably to a predicted 36% by 2030. Yet, under a regime of financial repression, this segment of society is exactly the group that would be expected to bail-out the reckless borrowers. This growing segment of society will be expected to face the financial repression "stealth tax" for a prolonged period of time. Will the pensioners accept negative real interest rates on their savings?

This represents a unique confluence in economic history and how it plays out will determine both the economic landscape as well as the investment opportunities. One might argue that the political cost of alienating pensioners (an important and growing segment of society) will cost governments popularity. Yet, faced with the various alternatives available, it may well be that financial repression is the only viable option that a government can consider. In many senses, the widespread adoption of quantitative easing measures by various governments has already tipped their hand as to how policy will unfold. This is not good news for the elderly, those living on pensions and savers at large.

Economic growth hits the debt buffers – the Debt Burden

The demographic headwind to financial repression is clear to see. A rising age-dependency ratio doesn't bode well for economic growth or for a government's ability to shrink an outsized budget deficit. It would be far easier for government to accomplish an effective financial repression when doing so would not risk a backlash from a major voting segment of society. Yet, demographics are only a part of the problem.

What if financial repression cannot achieve the aim of reducing the debt/GDP ratio because the scale of debt accumulation is so rapid that the repression cannot keep pace? According to the historical academic research, the impact of financial repression on the US and UK economies when it was applied amounted to an annual deficit reduction of 3-4% of GDP. That is a sizeable reduction. Yet, it may not be enough. According to the study entitled "Growth in a Time of Debt" by Reinhart and Rogoff for the American Economic Review in 2010, once the level of debt rises to above 90% of GDP, the economic growth rate of that economy becomes severely impeded. The study looks at over 44 countries spanning about 200 years of data. This amounts to over 3700 observations across a very wide variety of economic and political systems. The results, however, are very clear. Regardless of whether an economy is emerging or developed, once the ratio of government debt rises to above 90%, the rate of GDP growth achieved falls dramatically. For debt ratios below 90%, GDP growth for developed economies averages between 3.0-3.7%. For debt ratios above 90%, GDP averages just 1.7%. For emerging market economies, GDP growth averages between 4.1-4.3% for government debt levels below 90%, and just 1.0% for debt levels above 90%. The higher the level of debt ratio, the weaker the GDP growth outlook. It seems that this ratio holds true regardless of whether an economy is advanced or emerging.

In the past, this would have been an interesting but not especially relevant issue to consider when evaluating the bigger economic picture. In today's environment, however, it has become central to thinking. The following graph plots the proportion of OECD economies that had debt/GDP ratios above 100% in a particular year. This number was chosen as it is distinctly above the Reinhart and Rogoff threshold.

As can be seen from the graph, in the early 1980s, not one of the OECD economies had a debt ratio above 100%.

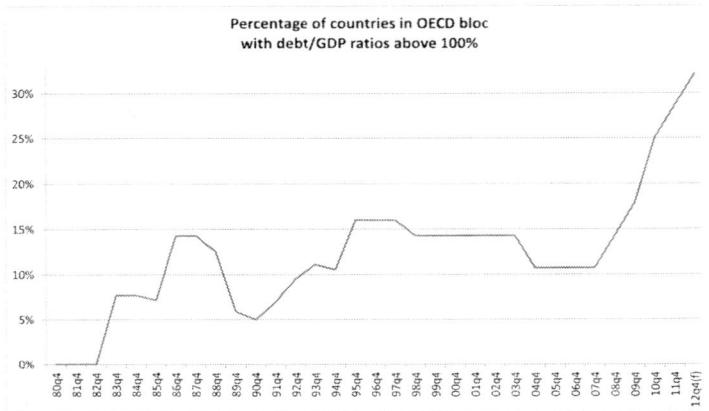

Throughout the 1980s and 1990s, the proportion of economies typically varied between 0-15%, averaging around 10%. So, out of 28 economies, one might have expected to see between 1 and 4 different countries with excess debt levels. According to the OECD, almost 30% of countries had debt ratios above 100% in 2011 and it is projected to rise to one-third of all OECD countries by 2012. Over the coming decade, then, there is a real possibility that for the first time in history, more countries within the OECD will have a debt liability in excess of the size of their GDP output than countries that do not.

A growing proportion of the OECD countries (including US, Japan, France and Italy) have debt ratios that are very likely to impede their growth prospects. The OECD estimates that the overall OECD debt/GDP ratio will surpass 100% for the first time ever in 2011. If growth is impeded, then in all probability the budget deficits of the OECD economies will rise. Cyclical increases in the budget deficits will, to varying extents, offset any improvements that might occur from financial repression. The bottom line is that if Reinhart and Rogoff's debt buffers at 90% do prove to be an impediment to GDP growth, then the level of debt that currently prevails in the OECD will make it very hard for governments to reduce their budget deficits through economic growth. Budget deficits will prove very hard to reduce and debt/GDP ratios will likely continue to edge upwards. This is one of the main findings from the Reinhart and Rogoff study:

> The sharp run-up in public sector debt will likely prove one of the most enduring legacies of the 2007-2009 financial crises in the United States and elsewhere....Seldom do countries grow their way out of debts.

Historically, it has been the emerging economies that have typically endured the financial crises, with runaway inflation, exploding debt ratios and currency devaluations. The tables have turned. The following graph is taken from IMF data, and shows that while advanced economies have seen a marked shift upwards in their government debt/GDP ratios, the emerging economies have actually seen their debt burdens fall. At least from a debt burden perspective, the emerging world does not have the same constraint to economic growth as is faced by the advanced economies.

Over the coming decades, then, advanced economies face a unique combination of rapidly rising age dependency (that has the potential to place enormous pressure on budget deficits) as well as a fiscal starting

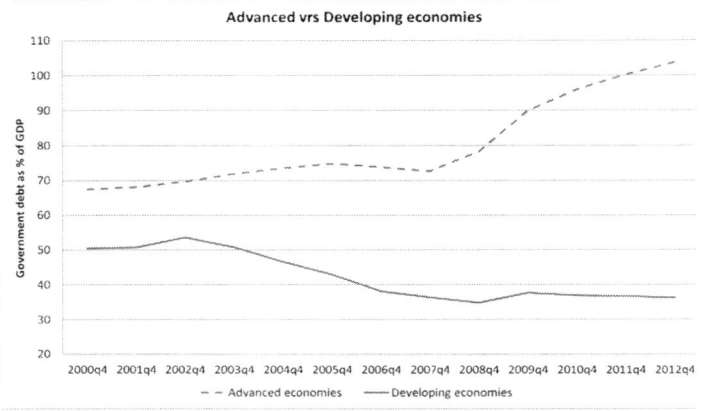

point where government debt/GDP is materially above a level that academic research suggests will impede economic growth.

Unlike the advanced economies (where promises are big and room for fiscal manoeuvre non-existent), emerging economies have materially lower debt/GDP ratios and appear to have a great deal more fiscal room to manoeuvre regarding their respective demographics. The picture for the advanced economies, then, appears quite grim.

Nobel Prize winner, James Tobin, was a staunch Keynesian economist. Yet, his study into the effects of running persistent budget deficits tends to support the conclusions of Reinhart and Rogoff. "The Monetary-Fiscal Mix: Long-Run Implications" (1986) describes a hypothetical economy with a persistent rise in the level of debt/GDP. Such a situation is not a million miles away from the current environment.

Tobin shows that for the first 11.6 years, no material observation can be made. Or as Tobin states "the visible penalties of gradual crowding-out are undramatic." However, as Tobin then shows, after 11.6 years the model hits an inflection point and a dramatic scenario unfolds. As Tobin describes it, a regime shift occurs.

Gradually but surely, the level of government debt overwhelms the financial markets to the point where no new investment takes place. After 23 years from the start of the experiment, Tobin's hypothetical model has seen the government absorb all private wealth and "the surviving capital stock is valueless." The rate of potential economic growth is persistently reduced from its initial trend rate.

So many Keynesian economists treat today's economic crisis as a lack of demand. To a man with only a hammer, everything looks like a nail. Borrow and spend is what created the problem. Applying the same as a cure will only make it worse. Tobin understood that, and clearly understood the potential catastrophe that could result should an economy enter a debt trap where levels of debt/GDP rise persistently. Amongst the OECD economies, the government debt/GDP ratio has already been rising persistently for well over a decade. These economies are now inside Tobin's zone of instability.

If one takes the Tobin analysis together with the Reinhart and Rogoff analysis, one can see that there is a neat meshing of thinking. According to both studies, debt/GDP can rise for a prolonged period of time before any negative effect materialises in the economy. Tobin suggested 11.6 years, whilst Reinhart and Rogoff set a specific debt ratio as an inflection point. What is clear from both studies is that there is *always* an inflection point, and that according to either yardstick, we are now inside that window of instability. According to Tobin's theory, then, we should also be seeing some impact on GDP growth rates. The following table is taken from the OECD 2011 Economic Outlook. The table looks at the OECD as a whole and also those economies that have seen the sharpest rises in debt/GDP ratios over the last decade.

Counties with the worst deterioration in debt/GDP levels over the last decade

Potential GDP (%)	Average 1989-98	Average 1998-2008	2011
US	3.1	2.6	1.9
UK	2.4	2.4	0.9
Japan	2.1	1.0	1.2
Portugal	3.2	1.6	0.5
Ireland	6.5	5.5	-0.3
Iceland	2.0	4.1	0.1
Greece	2.1	3.6	0.4
Average	3.1	3.0	0.7
OECD total	2.6	2.3	1.6

It would be very wrong to imply that this is "proof" that deteriorating debt/GDP ratios results in a deteriorating GDP potential. However, the evidence certainly does not conflict with that idea. Those countries that have seen the sharpest rises in debt/GDP ratio have indeed seen far more dramatic declines in potential GDP rates in recent years.

In an environment where the advanced economies desperately need to generate economic growth, the headwinds look ominous. Regrettably, the unique combination of demographics and debt are not the only problems that the advanced economies will need to address. Malthus has been proven wrong for many centuries. It takes a great deal for the world to run out of food. But eventually, every broken clock has its day (or at least moment) when it tells the right time. There is a good argument to be made that a lack of raw materials will prove to be a major fault-line threatening economic growth over the coming decade.

Supply constraints

The structure of the global economy has been changing dramatically. Up until the 1990s, the G10 economies of the world dominated global growth. Since that time, the industrialization of the developing economies has seen a new world order emerge with economies like Brazil, Russia, India and China (Jim O'Neill's BRICs) become the major drivers of global GDP.

In 1980, the advanced economies accounted for 69% of global GDP. In 1990, it was still at 69%. By 2000, it had fallen to 63%. In 2011, it stood at 52%. The following graph depicts this shift in economic power from the advanced economies to the developing ones.

As can be seen from this graph, the last decade has seen a dramatic shift. There is a new elephant in the room. One fairly certain bet is that those developing economies will continue to grow. According to the longer-term forecasts from *"Perspectives on Global Development: Shifting*

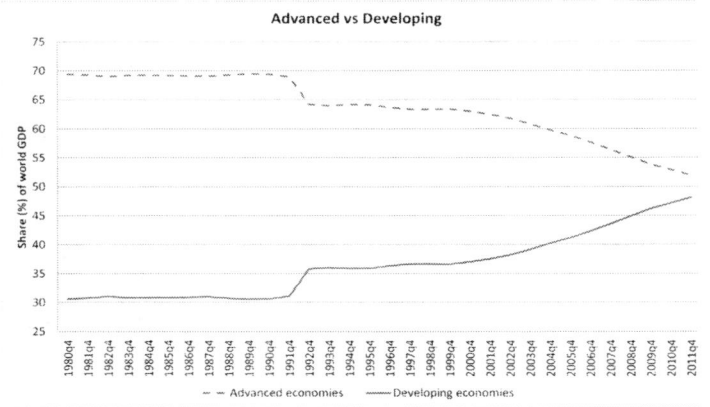

Wealth", a new publication from the OECD, today's developing and emerging countries are likely to account for nearly 60% of world GDP by 2030. If one looks at the level of GDP output per head, it can be seen that the developing economies have a significant gap to bridge before they have reached similar standards of living to the advanced economies. The following table shows the 2010 figures for GDP per head taken from the IMF World Economic Outlook Database (September 2011).

Country	GDP per head (using PPP)*
USA	$46,860
Germany	$36,081
United Kingdom	$35,059
France	$33,910
Japan	$33,885
Italy	$29,480

Country	GDP per head (using PPP)*
Russia	$15,612
Brazil	$11,723
China	$7,544
India	$3,408

*purchasing power parity

The BRICs are growing faster than the developed economies. Their share of global growth will almost certainly continue to rise for another 20 years or more. The gap in living standards between the BRICs and the developed world, however, is significantly large. In order to bridge that gap, the emerging economies will continue to strive to industrialise and develop the type of infrastructure that has allowed the advanced economies to prosper.

In itself, this shift in global power represents a major change in the macroeconomic landscape. However, for the purposes of the analysis here, the focus is on one particular facet of this shift; namely, the need for the emerging economies to consume raw materials in order to grow.

The following table shows a ranking of countries according to how much energy is consumed relative to how much output is produced relative to each economy. In economic jargon this is called energy intensity. The data is taken from Enerdata from their 2010 statistical energy review.

Country/Bloc	Energy intensity (koe$05p unit)
United Kingdom	0.10
Italy	0.10
Germany	0.12
Japan	0.12
France	0.13
Brazil	0.13
OECD	0.15
United States	0.17
India	0.20
Asia	0.22
Africa	0.25
China	0.28
Russia	0.32

As can be seen from the table, as a general rule, those countries that one would classify as emerging have higher energy intensity than the advanced economies. Another way of putting it is that those countries that are growing most are also the same countries that have the highest energy intensity. Demand for energy tends to correlate very closely with the rise in global real GDP. Regardless of the varying intensities of output, a generalised increase in global GDP tends to see an increase in energy consumption.

The US Energy Information Administration (EIA) provides excellent data on the subject of global oil production and consumption. The following graph looks at global consumption. The 2008/9 global recession can be seen, but notwithstanding that dip, the resumption in global GDP growth has seen global oil consumption rise to a new peak. In this sense, we are likely to see many more new consumption peaks.

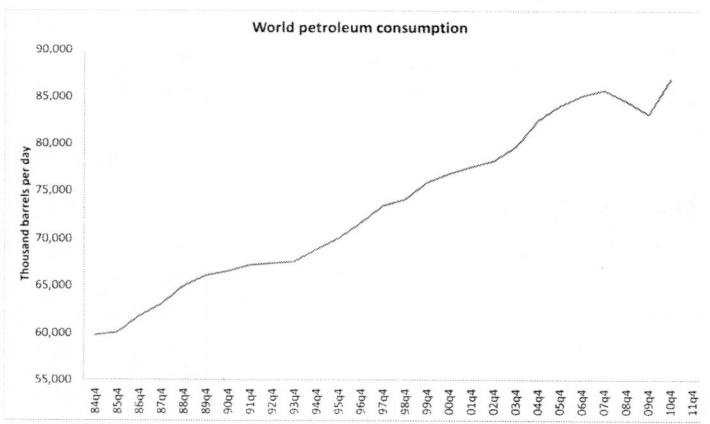

According to the EIA longer term projection, OECD consumption of oil over the coming 25 years or so is likely to grow by an average 0.2% p.a., whereas Non-OECD consumption is predicted to grow at 1.9% p.a. These projections are based on the oil intensity estimates for each country as well as their respective projected growth in real GDP. If one takes these forecasts at face value, then the OECD will be consuming 5% more oil in 25 years than it is now, but the non-OECD (emerging economies) will be consuming over 60% more oil. World demand for oil is predicted to be some 30% higher than currently.

To get some perspective on potential future energy usage, the EIA also provide regional forecasts across the entire energy spectrum (so including oil, natural gas, and other primary energy sources). The following graph plots the current usage of primary energy for the OECD bloc and the Non-OECD bloc and uses the EIA forecasts to project expectations across the two regions through to 2025.

So, as can be seen from the graph, the rapid expansion in the non-OECD (emerging) economies is predicted to drive a sharp increase in the consumption of all forms of primary energy over the coming decades.

The chart also shows that the non-OECD bloc has now become a bigger consumer of primary energy sources than the OECD. As global GDP continues to expand, energy consumption is likewise expected to continue to rise. The same picture is essentially true across the entire energy spectrum. Take natural gas. In 2008, the OECD

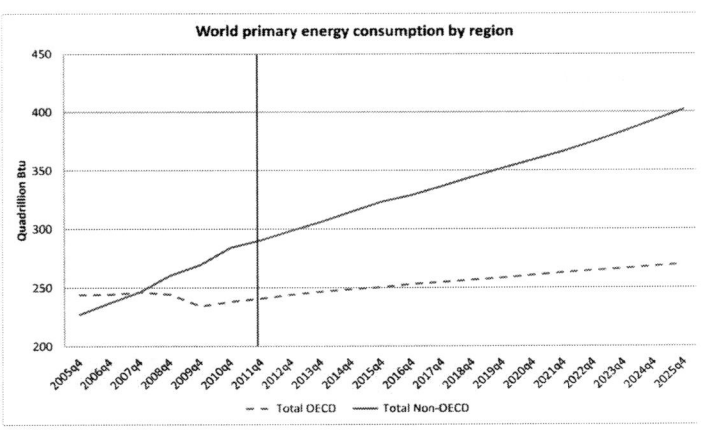

consumed 54.5 trillion cubic feet of it. By 2035, the EIA projects OECD usage to have risen to 68.5 trillion cubic feet – an increase of 25%. For the non-OECD bloc, consumption of natural gas in 2008 was 56.2 trillion cubic feet and it is projected to rise to 100.4 trillion cubic feet by 2035 – an increase of 79%. The demand for energy in its various guises is projected to increase significantly. Yet, it has been doing so for many decades already, so why is this a problem? Surely it indicates healthy projected economic growth?

Looking at the demand for such commodities is just a part of the story. The EIA also provide good statistics on energy production. The following chart is taken directly from the EIA and shows that since 2004 or so, world production of crude oil has been essentially static. Between 1994 and 2003, production grew at an annualised average rate of 1.5-2.0% per annum. Since 2004, growth has been essentially zero.

Now, it is not my aim to get into the complex debate of peak oil. My aim here is merely to point out the historical facts. Global demand has tended to rise each year as global GDP has risen. Realistic assumptions project that in 25 years' time oil consumption will be some 30% higher than it is today. Over the last 7 years, crude oil production has not really risen much at all. What is likely to happen when supply is fixed and demand rises? The quadrupling in oil prices over the last few years provides one answer. As the growth in the developing economies continues over the coming decade, should production of oil continue to display the static pattern of recent years, one can only anticipate

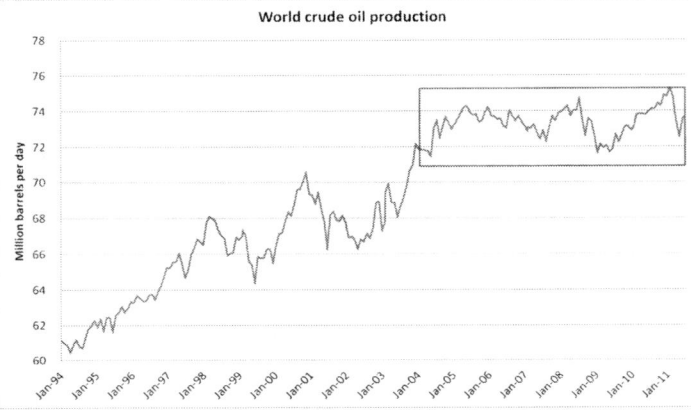

World crude oil production

more of the same in terms of higher oil prices. The arguments against peak oil are plentiful. Rather than indulge in an academic tit-for-tat on the subject, my purpose is merely to open up the possibility that oil prices will likely rise more and more as the emerging economies continue to industrialise. In a world of probabilities, this one certainly seems a good bet. The IMF certainly thinks so too.

The IMF has produced a detailed examination of the outlook for oil scarcity and what it might mean. Their report in the April 2011 World Economic Outlook provides a number of interesting points, but is summarised well in their following box:

> The increase in the trend component of oil prices suggests that the global oil market has entered a period of increased scarcity. The analysis of demand and supply prospects for crude oil suggests that the increased scarcity arises from continued tension

> between rapid growth in oil demand from emerging
> market economies and the downshift in oil supply
> trend growth. If the tension intensifies, whether from
> stronger demand, traditional supply disruptions, or
> setbacks to capacity growth, market clearing could
> force price spikes, as in 2007-08.

According to the IMF study, at current oil prices oil
consumption in China is projected to double by 2017
and triple by 2025. The IMF is quite clear in outlining its
concerns. The risks, according to the IMF report are that
*"there is a risk of larger-than-anticipated oil scarcity.
The possibilities range from larger downshifts in trend
supply to an outright decline in oil production, either
temporarily or more permanently."*

The IMF attempted to estimate what might happen to oil
prices if trend oil supply growth was reduced by 1%
below its historical trend. Such a forecast would not be
wildly different to that assumed by other major
forecasters. For example, BP (2011) and Shell (2011)
both predict low if any trend growth in oil production
over the medium-term. The IMF's benchmark
simulation suggests that oil prices would likely rise by
some 60% almost immediately and continue grinding
higher ever after.

The industrialisation of the emerging economies,
however, is not just about oil and energy demand. There
are strong arguments to be made to suggest that the
amount of raw materials left to be mined is much smaller
than many assume. According to Scientific American,

who ran a report in September 2010, at current levels of production and without recycling, "about 19 years' worth of silver remains in the ground." Work by Professors Reller and Graedel along with the US Geological Society was reported in the "New Scientist" in 2007 showing that many raw materials were effectively running out. The following table uses data provided in that New Scientist article.

No. of years of production left if:	1) The world consumes at today's rate	2) The world consumes at half the US consumption rate
Silver	29	9
Gold	45	36
Nickel	90	57
Zinc	46	34
Copper	42	8
Lead	61	38

Professor Graedel works at Yale University, specialising in areas of mineral sustainability. The study upon which the New Scientist article was based was, in many ways, reported badly. Graedel was really focusing on the current and future levels of demand for many raw materials. The reporting of the article leapt onto the implied supply constraints that are subsequently derived. Yet, understanding how much supply of any raw material is left in the ground is always going to be highly speculative. What was not speculative was the analysis conducted into the demand for raw materials, and it is this area that deserves much more attention.

According to the research by Graedel and Cao, "Metal Spectra as indicators of development", long-term demand for metals can be directly estimated from future GDP projections. Graedel confirmed the findings of Binder et al., namely that composite metal use is directly related to per capita wealth. In normalspeak, the more we grow, the more we use. The only reason the global economy may have a potential supply constraint is because demand is rising so sharply. According to Graedel's analysis, *the results suggest overall metal flow into use in 2050 of 5-10 times today's levels should supplies permit*. Imagine that. Up to 10 times the amount of silver will be needed each year by 2050. But, if below-the-ground supply will last for only 10-20 years, what will happen to price?

One can understand that it makes good headlines to run a story that suggests we are physically running out of raw materials. The truth of the matter is that these "supply constraints" issues are more about demand expansions. As China and other developing economies strive to reach standards of living commensurate with the developed nations, the demand for raw materials rises. Those raw materials have <u>always</u> been in fixed supply. Now, however, for many of those raw materials, the future demand will not be able to be met from below-the-ground resources. This is a key shift that many analysts do not fully understand. To get someone to scrap their silver teapot will require a significant increase in the price of silver. The drain on existing above-ground materials will become so intense as Graedel's 5-10 fold demand rise materialises that prices for such materials will rise very dramatically.

Gordon, Bertram and Graedel undertook a study in 2005 to evaluate metal stocks and sustainability. Some examples from their study are useful. The prognosis is that should the emerging economies of the world elevate their standards of living to the same level as the developed world, then global supplies of copper and zinc are not sufficient. The following is taken from their study:

Copper

A first-order application of the stocks-for-services hypothesis can be used to estimate future metal demand for copper by supposing that, as less-developed nations approach the level of services enjoyed by the developed nations, they will eventually require a similar level of metal stock per capita. The Intergovernmental Panel on Climate Change *Special Report on Emission Scenarios* (24) predicts a world population of 8.7×10^9 by ≈ 2050 and 10×10^9 to 15×10^9 by 2100. To provide each of 10×10^9 persons with a stock of 170 kg of copper, the per-capita average for North America (9), would require 1,700 Tg of copper. To attain this level of stock-in-use, more than the total world copper resource of $\approx 1,600$ Tg would have to be placed in a sustainable cycle. Even more copper would be required to attain the per-capita level of stock for the U.S. and other wealthy Western nations. Additionally, our data show that the

---

copper stock per capita in use in the U.S. continued to increase throughout the 20th century. No end to expansion of demand for copper services is yet in sight.

Zinc

The global zinc resource is estimated with less certainty than is the case for copper, but the U.S. Geological Survey gives 1,800 Tg of zinc as a working figure. The most recent estimate of in-use zinc stock in a wealthy country is ≈200 kg per capita. Were all of the world's peoples to employ zinc at the current wealthy country rate, and with contemporary technology, 2,000 Tg of zinc would be needed. Maintaining an in-use resource of this magnitude by cycling of the metal through different anthropogenic uses would be difficult so long as dissipative uses remain important in the ways in which zinc is used.

Two factors are going on here. First, there is the specific industrialisation process of the emerging economies that is requiring the need for large amounts of industrial metals in order to raise living standards to Western levels. Second, as the world economy grows, then the natural demand for metals will grow with it. Graedel's concluding points quotes Gordon et al:

Issues of sustainability now raise their heads, because the balance between demand and ultimate supply must be considered. Unlike fossil fuels, metals are not destroyed by use, though they may be dispersed or otherwise rendered unfit for reuse. Sustainability of supply is thus related both to mineable virgin ore deposits and to the eventual recyclability of metals. At present, few analyses of sufficient rigor and scope allow for confident assessments of metal sustainability, although Gordon et al state that providing today's developed world technological services for the world's population "would appear to require essentially complete extraction of copper ores and essentially complete recycling of copper exiting use." They suggest that the same could be true of zinc and the platinum group metals.

Peak oil? Peak metals? Again, the scope of this book is not to deal with balancing academic studies for and against such concepts. But rather to open the possibility that raw material costs have the potential to rise for the next decade as indeed they have for the last decade.

A simple conclusion drops out of this analysis. As these developing economies strive to bridge the wide gap between their respective standard of living and that already established by the advanced economies, the demand for raw materials like oil, copper, nickel, silver and lead will be driven hard. The emerging countries have a higher usage of raw materials precisely because they are still in the process of industrialising to the levels of the advanced countries. China ranks first globally in terms of its consumption of aluminium, copper, lead, nickel, zinc, coal, wheat, rice, palm oil and cotton. India ranks in the top 3 for consumption of coal, wheat, rice, palm oil, tea, sugar and cotton. In terms of raw material intensity, those countries that are growing fastest have the highest raw material intensities.

The growth of the emerging economies combined with their rising weight in global GDP combined with the clear potential for key raw materials to hit some wall of supply constraint opens the possibility that the coming decade will see a continuation of upwards pressure on commodity prices.

Now, in one sense, a healthy and growing emerging economic bloc is helpful to the global economy. However, in an environment where resources that are needed for growth are scarce, then higher prices for such resources will create another persistent headwind for growth for the advanced economies. Indeed, for economies that have no oil production capacity or countries that are totally reliant upon importing raw materials, the squeeze on profit margins that will result from much higher commodity prices will create a marked impediment to their ability to grow. This process has already been taking place for the last several years. One can expect it to intensify as that demand-supply imbalance persists.

The OECD bloc were fortunate to undertake most of their industrialisation when raw material prices like oil and copper were both cheap and abundant. The emerging economies will not have that luxury. Against all the points that can be said for the emerging bloc, supply constraints most definitely sit in that category of major negatives. For the advanced economies however, in a world where their debt burdens are excessive and where demographics weigh on both future growth expectations and fiscal repair, having to face the headwinds of sharply higher commodity prices will add to an already toxic cocktail of economic events.

The prescription for the advanced economies is financial repression. It is the most likely policy tool that can be used. Yet, the above toxic cocktail is likely to mean that the scale and depth of the cure needs to be greater than many assume. It is, perhaps, in this context that one needs to understand why so many central banks in the advanced economy bloc have adopted unconventional monetary policies such as quantitative easing. Against a backdrop where financial repression needs to be intense, the monetary response is crucial.

Bill Gross, of Pimco, manages the largest bond portfolio in the world. His monthly musings are one of the most widely read in the financial markets. His November 2011 report posed an interesting question:

> My original question - "Can you solve a debt crisis by creating more debt?" – must continue to be answered in the negative, because that debt – low yielding as it is – is not creating growth. Instead, we are seeing: minimal job creation, historically low investment, consumption turning into savings and GDP growth rates at less than New Normal levels. The Rogoff and Reinhart biblical parallel of seven years of fat followed by seven years of lean is not likely to be disproven in this cycle. The only missing input into the equation would seem to be how many years of fat did we actually experience? More than seven, I would suggest.

The origins of the current crisis had their roots in excessive borrowing. Gross is absolutely correct to question whether creating more debt is the cure. It is more like "hair of the dog" than cold turkey, and is more likely to create greater dependency on debt in the future. With all the headwinds that are set to be faced, the intensity of the future financial repression will need to be deep and prolonged. As Gross suggests, seven years of lean may be way too optimistic. But, as previously argued, most advanced economies have already tipped their hand as to how they will deal with the problem. Hair of the dog, it seems, is their choice.

Hair of the dog has proven itself workable from a political perspective before. Yet, the current economic landscape is different to anything that has been faced before. Very high government debt levels are not unique. Seeing such debt levels as *commonplace* across the OECD, however, is unique. Japan has been grappling with its demographic problems for well over a decade. But this is the first time ever that such demographic problems have become *commonplace* across the OECD. Peak oil has widely been seen as a possible constraint on growth. Yet, as the developing economies become the world's biggest driver of economic growth, the constraints on oil and other important raw materials will likely impact in a way that is difficult to envisage. Throughout most of the 1990s, oil traded at around $20 per barrel. By 2005 it had doubled to over $40 per barrel. By 2008 it had jumped to over $100 and today it is over $120. When supply constraints emerge, prices move dramatically. **What happens when three unique secular factors all emerge at the same time?**

Summary – Chapter 5

- Ageing demographics in the advanced economies will result in a sharp rise in the number of elderly relative to working population. As a result, there will be distinct upward pressure on governments to spend more and at the same time less people to tax. Growth expectations will be hurt by the forthcoming demographic dynamic. The rate of deterioration in this demography is now at an inflection point.

- Against this demographic backdrop, the need to generate strong economic growth is all the more necessary. Regrettably, the starting point for growth is with one-third (and rising) of OECD economies nursing debt/GDP ratios above 100%. As Reinhart and Rogoff contend, this debt hangover will present a strong impediment to economic growth.

- The growth in the EM bloc will drive key raw material prices higher. Demand for raw materials is rising in the emerging economies and supply is questionably fixed. A grab for resources is taking place and that represents a serious headwind to growth. The last thing the advanced economies of the world need on top of high levels of debt and an ageing population is a sharp rise in the cost of raw materials.

- Had one of these structural events been taking place, then the impact would still have been important for economic forecasting. However, when three such important and structural factors come together at the same time, all acting in the same direction, then the confluence has the potential to so radically change the economic outlook for the advanced economies as to make an examination of historical precedent impossible. Put simply, the advanced economies have never before been in this position. They've never had it so bad. Against this economic backdrop, the need for "intense" financial repression will be clear to governments.

CHAPTER 6

The Truth about Money Printing: Theory and Practice

Money printing in theory

I suppose it is quite easy to write a book by simply re-quoting passages written by other writers. One could argue that such a process is not really providing new ideas or thinking. However, in the context of this book, the following two pieces of analysis helped frame my thinking more than any others that I have read and by pulling them together have helped create new and different ideas. The first, by Murray Rothbard, helped create a framework for how central banks act and a way of thinking about what they do and its implications. The second, by Ben Bernanke, made concrete the theory espoused by Rothbard and set forward a plan for how to take advantage of the theory. Taken together, these two passages are, in my view, absolutely critical for any investor to understand. This chapter aims to expound on these two pivotal pieces of writing as it is upon this thinking that the theory of SWAG investing is based.

David Hume was a British classical economist who lived in the 1700s. As far back as the 1700s, Hume was postulating on the effect of money printing on inflation. Indeed, Hume should rightly be recognised as one of the first (if not the first) to put forward the quantity theory of money. Hume was one of the first Monetarists. Rothbard discusses Hume's thinking of the impact of money supply on inflation by what Rothbard calls the "Angel Gabriel Model." Rothbard goes on to explain:

> In this model, the Angel Gabriel after hearing pleas for more money from the mortals on earth magically doubled each person's stock of money overnight. .....It is clear that while everyone would be euphoric from their seeming doubling of monetary wealth, society would in no way be better off.
>
> As people rushed out to spend the new money, the only impact would be an approximate doubling of all prices, and the purchasing power of the money would be approximately halved, with no social benefit being conferred.
>
> Milton Friedman's more modern though equally magical version is that of his "helicopter effect", in which he postulates that the annual increase of money created by the Federal Reserve is showered on each person proportionately to his current money stock by magical government helicopters.

Rothbard goes on to point out that while we can assume benign motives for the Angel Gabriel, we cannot make the same assumption for a mere mortal. In real life, then, the very point of printing money (or counterfeiting as

Rothbard calls it) is to constitute a process of transmitting money from one pocket to another, and not the result of a magical and equi-proportionate expansion of money in everyone's pocket simultaneously. In reality, counterfeiting is always a process in which the counterfeiter gets the new money first. When that counterfeiter has a self-interest in printing more money, one can expect the process to occur.

As Rothbard goes on to explain:

> The first people to get the money are the counterfeiters, which they then use to buy various goods and services. The second receivers of the new money are the retailers who sell goods to the counterfeiters. And so on and on the new money ripples out through the system, going from one pocket to another. But as prices of goods begin to rise in response to the higher quantity of money, those who haven't yet received the money find the prices of goods they buy have gone up. In short, the early receivers of the new money in this market chain of events gain at the expense of those who receive the money towards the end of the chain, and still worse losers are the people who never receive the money at all. Monetary inflation, then, acts as a hidden "tax" by which all early receivers gain at the expense of the late receivers. This tax is particularly insidious because it is hidden, because few understand the process of money and banking, and because it is all too easy to blame the rising prices, or "price inflation" caused by the monetary inflation on greedy capitalists, speculators, wild-spending consumers, or whatever social group is easiest to denigrate.

The next component of Rothbard's analysis makes a crucial distinction between the typical understanding of monetary economics and the Rothbard version. As Rothbard explains:

> The big error of all quantity theorists, from the British classicists to Milton Friedman, is to assume that money is only a "veil", and that increases in the quantity of money only have influence on the price level, or on the purchasing power of the money unit. On the contrary....in addition to this quantitative, aggregate effect, an increase in the money supply also changes the distribution of income and wealth. The ripple effect also alters the structure of relative prices, and therefore of the minds and quantities of goods that will be produced, since the counterfeiters and other early receivers will have different preferences and spending patterns from the late receivers who are "taxed" by the earlier receivers.

Now, regardless of whether Rothbard is right to criticise other branches of monetary economics or not, the fact is that Rothbard draws attention to a very important issue. In sum, the Austrian School of Economics (espoused by Rothbard) holds that money printing (or counterfeiting) will have far more unfortunate consequences for the economy than simple inflation of the price level. Rothbard's analysis suggests that not only will there be a big timing difference between those that receive the benefits first and those that see them last, there will also be a difference created by the type of assets that are purchased by those that see the money first compared with those that see it later. The rich tend to have a lower propensity to spend. This means that if you gave a multi-millionaire a pay increase of £100 a week, most likely most of this pay increase would be channelled into savings rather than consumer spending. If the same £100 pay increase went to someone on a minimum wage, then the proportion of it that would most likely be spent on consumer goods and services is close to 100%. This point that is absolutely central to the idea of SWAG.

If your next-door neighbour secretly had a money printing machine and was secretly printing money, would you like it? Each day you would go out to work and put in honest labour. You would save in order to buy things that you wanted. Your neighbour was out partying each night and just printed more money so that he could buy himself a new car and take Caribbean holidays. Would you accept that situation? Yet, in reality, that is happening all the time as governments print (or should I say counterfeit) more money. It does not get redistributed in an even way. Someone wins. Someone loses. In theory, then, there are clear winners and clear losers. Even the Federal Reserve in the US has no issue on this point as the Federal Reserve Bank of St. Louis stated in 1975:

> The decrease in purchasing power incurred by holders of money due to inflation imparts gains to the issuers of money.

In a real-life scenario, then, determining who the early receivers of printed money are can reveal one of the key questions about the benefits of money printing. Obviously, as Rothbard describes, government are the very first receivers of printed money. They are the biggest winners. In today's world of finance, it is the banking system and those closely associated with it that see the money next as the central bank typically buys back government debt (and other assets) from the banking system.

Given that money printing is set to dominate central bank policy for the coming decade, understanding Rothbard's thinking of monetarism provides the central plank for planning an investment strategy.

Ben Bernanke cemented, for me, Rothbard's theory. The following text is taken directly from a speech by Ben Bernanke in November 2002. It looks at the problem that any central bank faces when interest policy rates approach zero and yet still a deflation threat approaches. Given Rothbard's thinking on money printing, Bernanke's illustration of how a modern day central bank deals with a specific economic problem is illuminating:

Let me start with some general observations about monetary policy at the zero bound, sweeping under the rug for the moment some technical and operational issues.

As I have mentioned, some observers have concluded that when the central bank's policy rate falls to zero - its practical minimum - monetary policy loses its ability to further stimulate aggregate demand and the economy. At a broad conceptual level, and in my view in practice as well, this conclusion is clearly mistaken. Indeed, under a fiat (that is, paper) money system, a government (in practice, the central bank in cooperation with other agencies) should always be able to generate increased nominal spending and inflation, even when the short-term nominal interest rate is at zero.

The conclusion that deflation is always reversible under a fiat money system follows from basic economic reasoning. A little parable may prove useful: Today an ounce of gold sells for $300, more or less. Now suppose that a modern alchemist solves his subject's oldest problem by finding a way to produce unlimited amounts of new gold at essentially no cost. Moreover, his invention is widely publicized and scientifically verified, and he announces his intention to begin massive production of gold within days. What would happen to the price of gold? Presumably, the potentially unlimited supply of cheap gold would cause the market price of gold to plummet. Indeed, if the market for gold is to any degree efficient, the price of gold would collapse immediately after the announcement of the invention, before the alchemist had produced and marketed a single ounce of yellow metal.

What has this got to do with monetary policy? Like gold, U.S. dollars have value only to the extent that they are strictly limited in supply. But the U.S. government has a technology, called a printing press (or, today, its electronic equivalent), that allows it to

> produce as many U.S. dollars as it wishes at essentially no cost. By increasing the number of U.S. dollars in circulation, or even by credibly threatening to do so, the U.S. government can also reduce the value of a dollar in terms of goods and services, which is equivalent to raising the prices in dollars of those goods and services. We conclude that, under a paper-money system, a determined government can always generate higher spending and hence positive inflation.

Bernanke spells out very clearly that the ability to produce endless pieces of gold would send the price down sharply. It is only gold's limited production potential that makes it valuable. US dollars, on the other hand, can be produced very freely at no particular marginal cost. By doing so, Bernanke points out that this will directly impact prices. In a world where higher prices can lead to a boost in nominal GDP, Bernanke has explicitly described the process by which the US Federal Reserve will deal with a debt-deflation risk. Bernanke has followed this policy script closely ever since.

Money printing in practice

The quote above is taken from Ben Bernanke's seminal speech in November 2002. In my view, it was the most pivotal moment of my career. Bernanke spells out a game-plan for how he would deal with a specific economic problem. And he could not have been clearer. If a debt-deflation became an issue, the Fed would engage a massive money printing process. <u>There would be a war on cash</u>.

What exactly is meant by a war on cash? In effect, it means that the government needs to devalue the buying-power of each unit of money so that it can pay off its debts at a cheaper rate. In other words, money printing is (as Rothbard explains) nothing more than counterfeiting where the counterfeiter in this instance is a legal counterfeiter, and the expropriation is about taking money from those that have (savers) in order to replenish the coffers of those that do not (the government). A by-product of this process is that the early receivers of the printed money tend to do very well out of the process. The early receivers are, invariably, the rich. They are rich because they know what money printing does and they know how to take advantage of it. They are rich because they know how to use the government's actions to invest in such a way that will benefit them significantly. They are rich quite often because they happen to position themselves to act in an area that is close to the early receivers of the printed money.

It is a key point that money printing benefits some sections of society above others. As Rothbard points out, classical economics fails to take account that when a central bank indulges in money printing (especially if that money printing is used directly to finance government over-spending), it has an effect not only on the general level of inflation but, specifically on specific segments of society and by implication on specific types of assets. An example may be useful.

Let's imagine that a central bank prints some money and uses that new money to buy back existing government debt. This process has a number of effects. First, the buying back of government debt has the initial effect of lowering government bond yields. This makes it cheaper for government to issue more debt and thus cheaper to stimulate the economy through fiscal policy. Lowering bond yields has a similarly stimulatory effect as borrowing costs are lowered. Second, the first to get access to the printed money will tend to be those closest to the source of the printing. If the central bank started buying up government debt (or indeed other types of bonds) from commercial or investment banks, those banks would suddenly find themselves with a lot of cash and less bonds. Recognising the policy stimulus taking place would lead them to re-invest the new cash in assets that would benefit from the stimulus to the economy that was taking place. Those working at those financial institutions would see first-hand the act of money printing and would be in pole position to act quickly by moving money into asset classes that would benefit. Interest rates get driven lower and stimulus gets injected into the economy. That is usually a good signal to invest in assets that would benefit from the impending price inflation.

But of course, there are many different ways that money printing can first find its way into the hands of the financially sophisticated. In November 2010, the Bank of Japan decided that it would start to purchase exchange traded funds that track the Japanese equity market and Japanese Real Estate Trusts. It is fairly clear who benefits quickly from the printing of money for such purchases, and it is not the unemployed worker on state subsidies. The early receivers in such scenarios will tend to be those with exposure to the assets that will benefit.

It must also be recognised that central banks are under no illusion as to what printing money does. They are completely aware that they are expropriating wealth from some in order to give to others. For those on pensions with fixed incomes, the expropriation is particularly painful. Such people see the buying power of their income shrink as their living costs rise, while others who have anticipated the inflation see the buying power of their assets rise. Historically, the process has been seen as one that takes from the prudent saver to bail out the reckless borrower. It creates a big division within society. Yet, when the party concerned in the equation is a government in debt, the printing press is seen as an acceptable means to re-allocate resources. Understanding this concept and taking advantage of it is what this book is all about. Nobody, it seems, can stop governments printing money but at the very least understanding the process can help insulate the prudent saver. So, according to theory, an expansion in the money supply has many different effects on the economy. Rothbard's brand of economics comes from the Austrian School of Thought. If Rothbard is correct, the printing of money not only causes inflation but also causes a re-distribution of wealth. That re-distribution of wealth underpins the strategy in this book. By understanding how that process happens and what to do to as a result is the rationale for why this book was written.

Rothbard argued that the re-distribution process typically benefitted the rich whilst the poor suffered most. It is important to understand if this premise is true and if so, how and why it happens. Andy Lees is an economist who used to work for UBS. I have never met Andy Lees, but have been an avid reader of his analysis for years. In a piece of research produced by Lees, it was argued that governments appear to be helping the poor by printing money. Yet, the inflation that is caused taxes the poor more than the wealthy, and thereby locks them deeper into the poverty trap. The poor then have to sell their services at cheaper and cheaper rates to cover the cost of servicing their debt whilst the rich have the tools to negate a lot of the inflation. Many thanks to Andy who allowed me to reproduce some of his thinking:

Printing money does however have one obvious winner; the financial sector. Printing money effectively transfers wealth from other parts of the economy, i.e. it is a tax on the real economy. Increasing the money supply has no direct impact on the output of the economy. There is simply more money against the same amount of GDP, but banks can use the new money to acquire assets before full-knowledge of the extra money supply has filtered through into higher prices. It is a Ponzi scheme. As long as the banks can add to the money supply, they can gain ownership of the real assets against that printing of money.

Lees then makes a crucial point:

A new study from the Kauffman Foundation.....has found that over the past several decades, the growth in size and importance of the financial sector has run in tandem with lower – not higher – rates of new business formation. In the 1980's, when Wall Street really took off, the number of new firms created fell, and in the 1990's, it plateaued and has been stagnant ever since". The Fed's cheap monetary policy of the last 30 or 40 years has meant it has been far easier to make money playing financial markets than real markets. That in turn has meant that Wall Street has sucked an ever increasing percentage of graduates and top talent into financial innovation and away from real innovation.....The problem is that these are the sort of people that are most likely to start the sort of dynamic job creating new companies that the US needs. No wonder economists like Nobel Laureate Edmond Phelps speculate that the financialisation of the US and subsequent dampening of entrepreneurship may be at the heart of the country's long term productivity slowdown.

To summarise this, Lees is postulating that money printing has led the financial sector to grow disproportionately, but that this has had a negative effect on the economy as a whole. Basically, money has been filtered into the financial sector to the cost of the rest of the economy. To test Lees thinking, I looked at the size of US financial sector as a percentage of the whole economy relative to changes in the money supply.

The graph shows that between 1934 and 1981, financial sector profits typically represented between 5-20% of total profits, averaging 13.5%. From the early 1980s onwards, however, the size of the financial sector grew

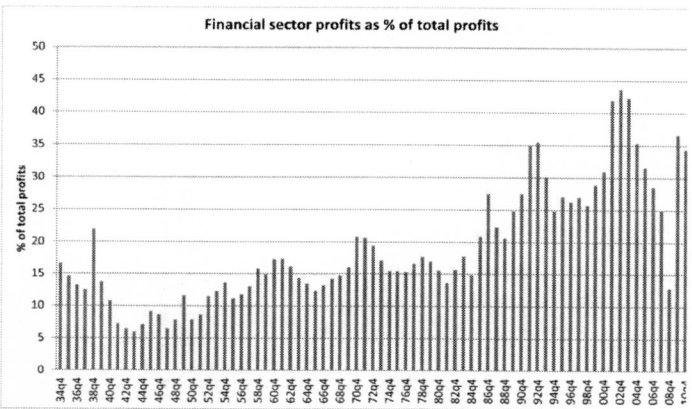

rapidly. At its peak in 2002/3, financial sector profits were almost half of the whole economy. Even after the credit crisis, financial sector profits still account for over one third of all profits. It is certainly a fair point to argue that the financial sector has been grabbing more and more of the profit cake.

The same picture emerges when looking at the financial sector as a share of the total business sector. Between 1934 and 1981, the financial sector's share of total corporate business GDP was between 4% and 8%, averaging just under 6%. The following plots the share of the financial sector in corporate GDP <u>since</u> 1981. It shows an inexorable rise in the size of the financial sector. Interestingly, its share of the output in the economy is much smaller than its share of the profits.

As the financial sector has grown in size and profits, so too have the bonuses and remuneration allocated to the employees in that industry. Indeed, as the size of the

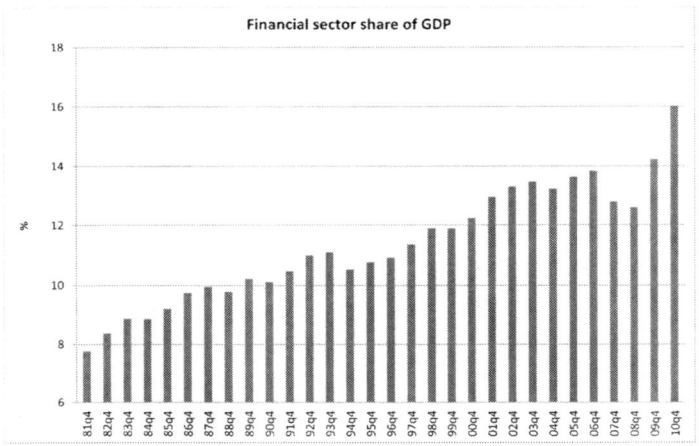

Financial sector share of GDP

financial sector has grown disproportionately, so too has the wealth allocated to its employees.

However, can this observation be pegged back to the expansion in the money supply? Regrettably, this is a very difficult question to answer. It almost becomes a jigsaw puzzle. If one looks at the expansion of the money supply in the US relative to the expansion in the economy (as measured by GDP), then it certainly seems reasonable to argue that money supply expansion has produced increasingly less and less real economic growth. Yet, if it hasn't produced meaningful economic growth and the financial sector has grown both in terms of its size in the economy and also its share of total profits, it isn't an unreasonable assumption to argue that the money supply expansion has been quite pivotal in underpinning the well-being of the financial sector.

If one looks at the changes in US money supply (M2) relative to GDP, it does appear that each extra dollar of money printing has produced less and less real economic activity. The following table aims to gauge that *bang-for-the-buck*. It looks at how much real GDP is created from each marginal dollar of M2. The number is indexed to the earliest data point that is used in 1964.

The marginal bang*	1964	1970	1980	1990	2000	2010
US M2	100	97	36	35	32	23

*The boost to GDP from an increase in the money supply

Put another way, each extra dollar of M2 now produces just under one quarter of the boost to GDP that it did in 1964.

As an academic exercise, the same process was applied to the global stock of money (as measured by global foreign exchange reserves excluding gold) relative to global GDP. On a global scale, it is also the case that money supply expansion is having a radically lower impact on real GDP growth. The bang for the buck appears to be getting less and less.

This would support Andy Lees contention that the expansion of the financial sector has had a negative effect on real GDP growth. Lees ties the expansion of the money supply in the US (and the commensurate rise in the financial sector) with the gradual decline in total productivity displayed by the economy. Again, this makes intuitive sense. The hard evidence supports the theory. The following table looks at total factor productivity for a number of economies over time. Total factor productivity is economist jargon for how efficiently stuff is made.

Total factor productivity %	Pre 1973*	1990-99**	2000-09**
US	1.5%	0.6%	0.3%
UK	2.1%	1.2%	0.1%
Japan	6.3%	-0.1%	0.2%
Italy	4.8%	0.4%	-0.8%
France	4.4%	-0.1%	-0.4%

*OECD Economic Studies No.10 1988
** US Conference Board Total Economic Database

Economics is full of false causality. Event A happens, then B happens then C happens, therefore A causes B that causes C. For so much in economics, causality is assumed as a given thing whereas in fact determining what causes an effect in a complex set of scenarios is an extremely difficult thing to prove. What we have here is a situation where more and more money supply growth has led to less and less GDP impact. Yet, at the same time, the financial sector has grown as a share of the economy and in particular with respect to its share of the profits. Simultaneously, the overall productivity in the economy has fallen step-by-step with the rise in prominence of the financial sector. Is there causality? To my mind, Lees conclusion makes sense. Proving it is another matter.

The process I describe above is a variation of Gresham's Law. This law was named after Sir Thomas Gresham, a sixteenth century financial agent to the English Monarchy. Gresham explained to Queen Elizabeth I that since her father Henry VIII had replaced 40% of the silver in the coinage with base metals, English merchants and a growing number of citizens would save the (good) old shillings from pure silver and hoard them, using the (bad) debased new shillings for transactions. The good shillings were hoarded and went out of circulation. This "law" became boiled down to a simple philosophy: bad money drives out good money.

Rothbard described Gresham's Law thus:

> When government compulsorily overvalues one money and undervalues another, the undervalued money will leave the country or disappear into hoards, while the overvalued money will flood into circulation. Hence the popular catchphrase of Gresham's Law: Bad money drives out good.

In Andy Lees example, the bad money (money printing) has been driving out good businesses allowing an expansion of the financial sector which takes full advantage of money printing, even indulging in the process itself. Good is driven out by bad. Total factor productivity falls as a result. Or, in layman's words, the economy starts to struggle.

As a result of this process, the economy becomes filled with "bad" businesses that have low productivity, that distort the distribution of wealth and allocate resources badly. Again, the Austrian School of Economics has a name for this process: Malinvestment.

"Malinvestment" is essentially any investment made by a company that is allocated badly due to an artificially low cost of credit and an unsustainable increase in money supply. Examples of such malinvestment might be the proliferation of real estate agents amidst the 2005-08 housing boom in the US or the number of SUVs sold on easy credit. Ludwig von Mises had his own way of describing it:

> The popularity of inflation and credit expansion, the ultimate source of the repeated attempts to render people prosperous by credit expansion, and thus the cause of the cyclical fluctuations of business, manifests itself clearly in the customary terminology. The boom is called good business, prosperity, and upswing. Its unavoidable aftermath, the readjustment of conditions to the real data of the market, is called crisis, slump, bad business, depression. People rebel against the insight that the disturbing element is to be seen in the malinvestment and the overconsumption of the boom period and that such an artificially induced boom is doomed. They are looking for the philosophers' stone to make it last.

In economics very little is provable. Causality is always questionable. Having said that, the Austrian School of Economics would contend that the expansion of the money supply over the last 30-40 years has resulted in widespread malinvestment. Certain businesses have thrived because of the easy credit that has been available and those businesses have grown disproportionately to the rest of the economy. Those who could take advantage of the easy credit (and certainly I would include the rich and creditworthy, the finance industry and real estate to name a few) have seen their relative wealth rise very quickly. One could argue that the entire sub-prime crisis in the US was a direct result of allowing credit in the form of cheap mortgages to be granted to those who had no realistic hope of servicing those mortgages. Notwithstanding all the financial crises of the last decade, the financial sector has been a very big winner from the monetary policy advocated over the last several decades. But it has come at a cost, and that cost has probably been the loss in productivity in the economy.

The irony to this is that as the productivity of the economy gets crowded out more and more by the proliferation of the financial sector, and as the economy struggles to generate any growth at all, the central banks determine that boosting the money supply via quantitative easing is the solution. This is akin to feeding the weeds in a garden so that eventually the roses are strangled out of existence. Yet, that is exactly the policy being pursued by the central banks. Obviously, my own bias in this is that the policy is absurd. Yet, having said that, I believe that as an investor one needs to look at what will work rather than what governments *should* do. In a world where central banks believe more money printing is the solution to (rather than the cause of) the problem, an investor needs to develop a strategy to deal with that reality. The rich have always understood that.

Summary Chapter 6

- When a central bank prints or "creates" money, it constitutes a process of transmitting money from one pocket to another. If a private individual printed (counterfeited) money that was indistinguishable from legal tender, then the big winners in that process would be the counterfeiter and then all the places where the counterfeiter spent that money.

- One of the big contributions from Austrian economics is the idea that when money is printed by a central bank, the effect that it has on specific segments of society are very different. There are clear winners and clear losers. Government are the very first receivers of printed money. They are the biggest winners. In today's world of finance, it is the banking system and those closely associated with it that see the money next as the central bank typically buys back government debt (and other assets) from the banking system.

- Between 1934 and 1981, US financial sector profits typically represented between 5-20% of total profits, averaging 13.5%. From the early 1980s onwards, however, the size of the financial sector grew rapidly. At its peak in 2002/3, financial sector profits were almost 50% of the whole economy. Even after the credit crisis, financial sector profits still account for over one third of all profits.

- *His November 2002 speech showed that Ben Bernanke understood fully the implications of printing money; "Like gold, U.S. dollars have value only to the extent that they are strictly limited in supply. But the U.S. government has a technology, called a printing press (or, today, its electronic equivalent), that allows it to produce as many U.S. dollars as it wishes at essentially no cost."*

- It is a reasonable argument to tie the expansion of the money supply (and the commensurate rise in the financial sector) with the gradual decline in total productivity displayed by an economy. In economic jargon, the economy becomes embedded with "malinvestment". Malinvestment is any investment made by a company that is allocated badly due to an artificially low cost of credit and an unsustainable increase in money supply. Examples of malinvestment might be the proliferation of real estate agents amidst the 2005-08 housing boom in the US or the number of SUVs sold on easy credit.

- The Austrian School of Economics would contend that the expansion of the money supply over the last 30-40 years has resulted in widespread malinvestment. Certain businesses have thrived because of the easy credit that has been available and those businesses have grown disproportionately to the rest of the economy. Those who could take advantage of the easy credit (and certainly I would include the rich and creditworthy, the finance industry and real estate to name a few) have seen their relative wealth rise very quickly.

- But where there are winners, there are also losers. Historically, the process of money printing has been one that takes from the prudent saver to bail out the reckless borrower.

CHAPTER 7

The Best Fund in the World

The sad truth is that there are really only two *solutions*
to the current crisis, and neither of them is pretty. A debt
default scenario will emerge if a sovereign is unable to
pay its debt obligations. The Eurozone looks the most
likely culprit. The UK or US always have an option to
print more of their domestic currency so that a default in
local currency terms is avoided. The Eurozone doesn't
necessarily have that option. If Spain or Italy can't pay
their debts it is by no means certain that Germany will
sanction a mass-printing of Euros to debase the problem
away. Regrettably, if a sovereign state the size of Spain or
Italy defaults in this way, it will bust not only European
banks but almost certainly the global financial system.
So, even for countries that can debase the problem away
(i.e. allow nominal GDP to grow courtesy of inflation),
the solution may be de-railed by an extraneous default
inside Europe.

A major sovereign debt default would be a catastrophe
for global markets. A generalised inflation that saw
nominal GDP rise faster than debt accumulation would
be the politician's solution of choice. Yet, the problem

being faced now is that a debt default is not with a small company, but a handful of the world's largest economies and that would cause a debt default chain-reaction. Hoping for real economic growth to solve the problem just isn't on the table of options. As unpalatable as it may seem, there really isn't a happy ending possible now. Default will occur one way or another; either through actual default or by what I call back-door default where inflation rises sharply.

So, the bad news is that for equity investors, bond investors and those hoping to earn a living from their cash, there is a very poor prognosis ahead. The structure of the political system, the nature of the public debt overhang and the risk of a sovereign default contagion make investment in traditional assets unpalatable. The good news is that policy makers have tipped their hand as to their choice of solution. In an environment where money printing is rife, investors need to invest in a fund that will provide them with a return that takes account of the risk. Fortunately, there is such a fund.

Investment in this fund has provided outstanding returns. Using data from the Barclays Capital Equity Gilt study, it can be seen that since 1925, US equities have produced an average annualised return of around 5.5% with a standard deviation around that average of about 20%. The UK equity market has produced marginally higher returns of 5.7% but with slightly higher volatility. In layman's terminology, this means that an investor can expect his returns to fall in a range of -35% to +45% with about 95% confidence. That is some reassurance.

My mystery fund has produced an annualised return of 6.3% per annum with substantially lower volatility. In fact, the mystery fund has about one quarter of the volatility of the overall equity market. $100 invested in the US equity market in 1925 grew to just short of $10,000 by 2010. £100 invested in the UK equity market grew to just over £10,000 by 2010. If the same $100 (£100) had been put into my mystery fund, it would have grown to over $16,000 (£16,000). It would also have generated a lot less anxiety.

Since 1970, the worst three year performance of the mystery fund was a positive return of 4%. The US and UK equity markets have seen several bouts where returns have been down between 20% and 40% over a 3yr period. The following graph depicts the return profile for each of the investments, indexing them all to the same 100 level back in 1925.

Of course, I am playing a trick. The mystery fund is none other than the US money supply, M2. However, the point

is a valid one. If it was possible to invest in a fund that mimicked the money supply, then almost certainly there would be many investors wanting some of that action! Such a fund does not exist, however finding assets that in some way capture the effect of that rise in the money supply is a very good objective. This is something that certain investors - the rich - have always understood.

When I was at University, one of my closest friends once accused me of having more money than sense. I spent my time during the holidays working so tended to have a little more cash than the average student, and I tended to live a little better as a result. I was stung by my friend's comment. Then I thought about it. It actually wasn't an insult at all. It was a compliment. If I had more money than was commensurate with my level of intelligence, then I was clearly punching above my weight. If my intelligence level was actually low, but I had a load of money, then surely that is a great result. On the other hand, if my intelligence level was high, then that would mean I was even richer. Another great result. Having more money than sense was definitely a compliment. What I most definitely did not want was to have less money than sense. That would really not be good.

What exactly does this have to do with an investment strategy to deal with the current market environment? Actually, quite a lot. The "Rich" have always been seen to be somewhat frivolous, paying huge fortunes for seemingly obscure and often absurd pieces of art. Owning art is quite often seen by society at large as somewhat pretentious and in many cases based on social climbing. "Darlings, you must simply come over to look

at our Picasso". It is a way for the social climber to
show his wealth on his wall. Wine is a similar asset. It is
viewed somewhat negatively by the masses as something
that the rich buy, yet probably couldn't differentiate
between a Chateau Lafite and a Bulgarian Bull's Blood.
The buyers of such assets are scorned for having more
money than sense. Spot on. They absolutely do have
more money than sense, and that is a very good thing as
it has turned out.

Far from being frivolous and pretentious, the buyers of
such assets are acting in a very logical and shrewd way.
Throughout history, governments have periodically
reached points similar to today's problems and have
needed to extract wealth from those that have wealth.
Throughout history, the wealthy families that have
retained their wealth have learnt that they need ways to
guard that wealth against the likely actions of
government and those who would take their wealth from
them. Far from being frivolous, assets such as art have
provided the rich with a way of guarding their wealth.
The reason for this is because assets such as these have a
neat characteristic of mimicking the money supply. In
many ways, the objective of SWAG is to attempt to build
an asset class that mimics the expansion in the money
supply.

Summary Chapter 7

- There appears to be a clear mantra for many OECD governments. When in trouble, print money. Since so many OECD governments persistently spend more than they earn in revenues, they need to print quite a lot. There are, supposedly, only two certainties in life; death and taxes. Money printing comes under the latter.

- If only one could invest in the money supply. It grows faster than the equity market. It is less volatile than the equity market. It rarely ever falls. What a great investment. Imagine that – an investment that outperforms equities with less volatility and very limited downside.

- Whether by luck or shrewdness, over the centuries many investors have realised that mimicking the money supply is a good investment methodology.

- But how does an investor mimic the money supply? Although SWAG stands for Silver, Wine, Art and Gold, the acronym stands for any asset class with a set of specific characteristics. The aim is to provide assets with strong long-term capital preservation qualities that will be insulated against both the potential ravages of the economy and more specifically against the attack on purchasing power that arises from money printing.

CHAPTER 8

The SWAG Principles

Over a decade when equities have put in their worst performance since the 1930s and where government bond yields are at generational lows, it struck me that certain assets had very much bucked the trend. This got me thinking about asset classes generally and just what it is that differentiates one asset class from another. Some assets, in particular, stood out to me as ones that had performed especially well over the last decade or so. The performance was even more astounding given that over the last decade or so we have seen the busting of the internet bubble in 2000-02, a subsequent recession, the emergence of the US sub-prime crisis in 2007/8 that almost brought the world's financial system to its knees, a subsequent near-depression and now the emergence of a sovereign debt crisis in Europe. As economic problems go, it hasn't been an uneventful decade. Despite (though plausibly because of) such economic headwinds, Silver, Wine, Art and Gold have put in superb price performances. These assets have punched way above their weight. The SWAGs.

Guy, a lawyer friend of mine, called me up a few months ago to tell me about an article he had read. Apparently, the best performing wine over the last 20 years when held for a 5 year period was a 2004 Carruades de Lafite. This wine had appreciated by 3000-4000% over the defined 5 year holding period. Starting at £140 a case, it reached a price of over £4500. Notwithstanding the peculiarities of Carruades de Lafite, fine wine has exhibited a very strong asset performance over the last decade. The Liv-Ex fine wine index is up around 250% over the decade.

The story for Gold is well-known. From the low point of $250-300 a decade ago, where Gordon Brown decided it was in the country's best interest to sell the UK's holding of gold, gold has appreciated some 600-700%. Silver has put in a similar performance.

Art is a tougher asset to nail. All-time records are being set at Christies and Sotheby's for Picassos, Moores, Hepworths, Rodins and other such classic artists. The more well-known and prestigious the piece of art, the greater the price appreciation appears to have been. The Artprice Global Index takes an average, and shows that fine art as a whole has appreciated by 120% over the last decade.

Obviously, the nature of each asset has its own fabric and character, but they all share a similar characteristic. Namely, notwithstanding two global recessions, a severe global banking crisis, a credit crunch and (generally speaking) highly volatile and mostly negative equity market performance, they have all appreciated quite sharply with a relatively limited volatility given the size of their appreciation. The FTSE All-share index (and the

S&P500), by comparison, stands almost at the same level as a decade ago.

If held within a portfolio, the SWAG assets have provided a tremendous boost to an otherwise lacklustre portfolio mix of equities and bonds. Should SWAGs be an asset class in themselves? I believe there is some merit in thinking about allocating a portion of any portfolio to the SWAG grouping.

But what is it about the SWAG that allowed its investment performance to be so strong and so uncorrelated to mainstream asset classes? One way of looking at this question is to identify the common traits of each of these SWAG assets. What do they all have in common?

1) They are all physical assets that have longevity – Chateau Lafite will last for 50-100 years
2) They all have a ready market of exchange; demand is multinational
3) There is no incumbent debt associated with the asset
4) They are transportable and relatively easy to store/hold
5) There is scarcity – a finite supply
6) There is a relative uniformity of product – one case of Chateau Margaux 2000 is virtually identical to another. One kruggerand is virtually identical to another.
7) There is no income stream – so no income tax liability
8) Asset performance seems relatively uncorrelated to equity markets

9) A sovereign default would not alter any of the above traits

10) SWAGs have no specific currency of denomination

SWAGs, it seems, all carry a similar DNA. I am a big believer in the idea that no asset class is too risky. Risk is virtually ALL in the size of the allocation to an asset. Given the scale of the price increases in SWAGs, it seems sensible to me to have an allocation to them in a portfolio in one guise or another. Each of these assets can be used in a financial or portfolio capacity and is open to the small investor as well as the institutional investor.

I have read the views of many economists who tend to class SWAG-style assets as not "proper" assets because they have no income stream. Such thinking is tremendously naïve. To define an asset as needing an income stream fails to appreciate the very essence of an asset. Similarly, many economists argue that assets such as SWAGs cannot be valued objectively because they have no income stream. Well, again, I see that as short-sighted bordering on intellectually lazy. Analysts have no problem in valuing an equity that pays no dividend based on its P/E ratio. Why can't the SWAGs be valued on a similar basis? What is the P and what is the E, I hear the sceptical economists saying. Well, the P is the price of the asset, and the E? Well, that is the global money supply. As the global money supply rises and with real interest rates across the industrialised world negative, then the SWAGs get driven up in price. The more money printing there is, then the more investors will look to protect and insulate their investments by allocating to assets that have SWAG qualities. This is the reason that SWAGs deserve to be a part of any portfolio. The dangers that investors face from money printing now need to be actively addressed. The following chapter aims to look at each of the SWAG traits in the context of how classical economists view money and examines why each trait is important.

Summary Chapter 8

- Over a period when many traditional asset classes have performed very poorly, a number of alternative assets have bucked that trend. Despite two recessions, a collapse in the banking system and on-going concerns of sovereign default, Silver, Wine, Art and Gold (SWAGs) have recorded very strong returns over the last decade.

- SWAG assets tend to share a similar list of traits. In many senses, this list is important not because of its similarities with the classical traits of money, but rather because of the differences.

- The ten rules of SWAG can be summarised as;

  1) They are all physical assets that have longevity
  2) They all have a ready market of exchange; demand is multinational
  3) There is no incumbent debt associated with the asset
  4) They are transportable and relatively easy to store/hold
  5) There is scarcity – a finite supply
  6) There is a relative uniformity of product
  7) There is no income stream – so no income tax liability
  8) Asset performance seems relatively uncorrelated to equity markets
  9) A sovereign default would not alter any of the above traits
  10) SWAGs have no specific currency of denomination

CHAPTER 9

SWAG as Money

SWAGs, then, are a form of money with a twist. A typical economic definition of the word "money" puts forward three distinct uses. These uses are;

- A Medium of Exchange
- A Unit of Account
- A Store of Value

Economics goes on to define six characteristics that any item must have if it is to be considered a valid form of money. These six characteristics are;

1) Durability
2) Portability
3) Divisibility
4) Uniformity
5) Limited supply
6) Acceptability

It is quite easy to see that US dollar, Euro or Pound sterling all fit most of the categories above. However, more and more of these six characteristics are becoming abused by governments to the extent that the printed money that is supposed to represent something of value is becoming questionable.

Assuming that some standard of technical competence is a given, governments can be relied upon to create money that is durable, divisible and uniform. Any government should be able to manage that. However, the more nebulous areas of portability, supply and acceptance are areas that are now more questionable.

Portability

Let's imagine that I want to buy some chocolate. I take my money to the shop and exchange it for the chocolate. There is nothing questionable in that measure of portability. Yet, let's now imagine that I want to buy something expensive when I am on holiday. There are strict limits on how much "cash" can be taken abroad. Whenever one makes wire payments, the bank requirements on making such transfers are now becoming more onerous. If an economic crisis really did emerge, it would be entirely reasonable to assume that governments might impose capital controls that prevented money leaving the domestic economy. It is certainly the case that restricted capital controls have been in place before and should the current economic crisis take a particular turn for the worse, such controls will almost certainly be put in place again. Having wealth stored in money/currency balances may provide very little portability in such circumstances.

Acceptability

If Greece was not a part of the Euro, its problems would most likely have been reflected via a much weaker

Drachma. In situations where a sovereign balance sheet is so clearly impaired, the acceptability of that sovereign's currency diminishes very quickly. There are literally hundreds of examples of economies that have found themselves to be technically bankrupt and the only way to avoid default on their own domestic debt is to print more money to pay off their creditors. Such situations often lead to very high levels of inflation and rapidly depreciating exchange rates. With balance sheets across the OECD now severely impaired, and with budget deficits still enormous in the absence of economic growth, many OECD economies are now resorting to aggressive money printing. The acceptability of their respective currencies will become more and more questionable.

Supply

Acceptability and supply are, in this instance, different sides of the same coin. It would be a joke to suggest that governments are maintaining a strict control on the supply of money. Rather the opposite. As economic growth has failed to materialise, OECD governments have decided to embark on a monetary experiment that has a very uncertain outcome. Unlimited supply of money does not really fit into the standard definition of stable and sound money.

SWAG – a new definition of money

The short-listed traits of SWAGs below are, in many ways, similar to the classic characteristics of money.

1) They are all physical assets that have longevity – Chateau Lafite will last for 50-100 years (durability)

2) They all have a reasonably ready market of exchange (acceptability)
3) Demand for the asset is cross-border - multinational demand (acceptability)
4) They are transportable and relatively easy to store/hold (portability)
5) There is a relative uniformity of product (uniformity)

SWAGs, like printed money, share a number of similar characteristics. Printed money clearly has the edge on many issues. One couldn't turn up at the supermarket and offer a bottle of Lafite in exchange for the groceries. But, by and large, SWAGs do appear to share a number of similar qualities. The importance, however, is in the differences.

Limited Supply

SWAGs are unable to have their supply expanded in an unlimited Quantitative Easing-style manner. Rodin only produced so many sculptures. There are only so many cases of Chateau Lafite 1996 left...and each day less and less of it. Gold and silver clearly do see more supply as mining output rises, but the extent of that increase in supply is physically limited. In a crisis that sees the money supply expand rapidly, SWAG supply will remain virtually constant. In this sense, SWAGs will always become relatively scarcer in relation to an expanding stock of printed money, especially when the latter's supply gets boosted through quantitative easing.

SWAGs carry no incumbent debt

SWAGs do not carry with them any incumbent debt. When you buy an asset that has attached to it an associated debt, one runs the risk of default should the associated debt become un-payable. I have known many people become very wealthy by accumulating a large property portfolio underwritten by significant mortgage borrowing. It works beautifully when property prices rise and when tenants are paying their rent. But the moment that property prices start to fall and/or tenant vacancies rise, the vulnerability of the asset gets exposed by the underlying leverage or borrowing that sits with it. Many assets can carry this type of incumbent debt, and it is generally something that can create wild swings in the performance of the asset. One could argue that the entire credit crunch that enveloped the US housing market was driven by this issue. SWAGs tend to be free of this type of problem.

SWAGs have no specific currency of denomination

A krugerrand is not denominated in any specific currency. Nor is a case of Chateau Lafite. Nor for that matter a work of art. There is no base currency. This is another crucial component of a SWAG and one that differentiates it, by definition, from printed currencies. Perhaps the best way to demonstrate this point is by way of a stylised example.

Let's imagine there are three art collectors looking to buy a very specific Henry Moore sculpture. The sculpture in question is in a limited edition of 6 pieces and the last time one came up for auction was 20 years ago. In a month's time, Christies are due to auction a wide range of 20th Century Art, and this particular Henry Moore piece is going to be one of the lots. The guide price for the piece is £100,000 or $160,000 or EUR 120,000. The respective exchange rates being £/$ 1.60, £/Eur 1.20.

The three collectors are respectively based in London, Paris and New York. The auction takes place and the New York bidder outbids the other two and takes the piece for $160,000. Both the British and French collectors would have been willing to pay the equivalent of $160,000, but the American got there first and neither British nor French wanted to pay more. Over the course of the coming year, the UK economy suffers another downturn and the government and Bank of England decide to initiate another burst of quantitative easing. This results in a uniform 25% weakening in the pound against all currencies. The New York collector becomes worried about another crisis in the US and decides he wants to sell the Henry Moore (clearly hasn't read this book yet). Art prices over the year have remained relatively static and Christies inform the New York seller that he can expect a price similar to what he paid.

When the piece is re-auctioned, the Parisian bidder is happy to pay the same price that it was initially sold for of $160,000, which was the equivalent of EUR 120,000. The British bidder, however, couldn't compete because his pounds were now worth so much less. He would have needed to pay £125,000 now (compared with £100,000 initially) for the piece. In USD or EUR terms, the Henry Moore has not changed price. But for the British collector, it now costs him a lot more pounds to buy exactly the same sculpture.

Where an asset can be housed in any country, and where it does not have an embedded currency of denomination, and where the number of people interested in the asset is spread across the world, the asset effectively takes on a currency denomination of its own.

In an economic environment where each government wishes to provide as much stimulus to its domestic economy as possible, policy mixes that encourage a weakening currency tend to be quite common. With higher inflation seen as a reasonable trade-off for lower unemployment, a weakening exchange rate is often seen as a reasonable policy choice. The trouble is, when ALL governments want to do the same thing, not ALL currencies can weaken. It is a zero sum game. In such a scenario, governments seemingly need to try to expand their own money supplies more aggressively in order to ensure that their domestic currencies weaken. The following is an extract from the statement made by former Swiss National Bank Governor, Philipp Hildebrand on 6th September 2011:

> The Swiss National Bank is therefore aiming for a substantial and sustained weakening of the Swiss franc. With immediate effect, it will no longer tolerate a EUR/CHF exchange rate below one Swiss franc twenty. The SNB will enforce this minimum rate with the utmost determination. It is prepared to purchase foreign exchange in unlimited quantities.

"Unlimited". That is quite some statement.

From an investor's perspective, holding assets in a currency that is expected to depreciate is not an optimal outcome. It is in this type of scenario that SWAGs hold their own. They have global demand, and because they are in such scarce supply, bidders from countries with strong exchange rates will find it relatively easy to bid for them. High quality assets gravitate to strong and prudent buyers. Printed money gets into trouble when its supply expands too aggressively. This leads to specific currency risk. SWAGs never have this problem. SWAGs are money, but money with backbone. Printed money so often has the backbone of a jellyfish.

Summary Chapter 9

- Economics defines six characteristics that any item must have if it is to be considered a valid form of money. These six characteristics are; durability, portability, divisibility, uniformity, limited supply, and acceptability.

- SWAG assets share a number of such characteristics with traditional forms of money. It is where SWAGs differ from traditional forms of money that is relevant in this context.

- **SWAGs are unable to have their supply expanded in an unlimited Quantitative Easing-style manner.** In a crisis that sees the money supply expand rapidly, SWAG supply will remain virtually constant. In this sense, SWAGs will always become scarcer in relation to an expanding stock of printed money, especially when the latter's supply gets boosted through quantitative easing.

- **SWAGs do not carry with them any incumbent debt.** When you buy an asset that has attached to it an associated debt, one runs the risk of default should the associated debt become un-payable. Many assets can carry this type of incumbent debt, and it is generally something that can create wild swings in the performance of the asset. One could argue that the entire credit crunch that enveloped the US housing market was driven by this issue. SWAGs tend to be free of this type of problem.

- **<u>SWAGs have no specific currency of denomination.</u>** A krugerrand is not denominated in any specific currency. Nor is a case of Chateau Lafite. Nor for that matter a work of art. There is no base currency. This is another crucial component of a SWAG and one that differentiates it, by definition, from printed currencies.

CHAPTER 10

SWAG in a Portfolio

SWAG assets are not just silver, wine, art and gold. The acronym could legitimately cover a broad range of qualifying assets (Appendix 1). However, the principle behind the acronym is relatively fixed. In a world where many advanced economy governments are effectively bankrupt, they will seek to avoid that bankruptcy by taking from others. That process can come in many forms. Money printing is a war on cash. It devalues the buying power of cash, and is nothing more than a theft by government of one's standard of living. It is legalised counterfeiting. But, if a government were facing the redemption of one of its bonds and literally had no revenues with which to make the payment, they could simply just print more money to make the payment. Who is the loser? Anyone who holds the cash denominated in that currency.

An alternative form of procuring the booty is by simply confiscating it. Nationalisation, taxation, and physical confiscation are all different types of angles employed by governments aiming to grab cash. One hears of political parties discussing "window taxes" and "garden taxes."

In effect what they are doing is taking from those who have to give to those that do not – in this instance, a government.

Governments have been in the business of this type of expropriation for thousands of years. The result has been that the rich have needed to evolve. In order to preserve wealth, the rich have needed to focus their attention on assets that somehow fly under the radar from government attention. Huge country houses just do not do the trick.

However, in this type of macro environment, it is not just the rich that need to protect their assets. All segments of society need to protect their assets, and that includes how portfolio and investment managers manage pension funds, insurance funds and endowment funds. It includes anyone with a self-managed pension and anyone with savings at all. Perhaps, most poignantly, those who would suffer most from financial repression.

At first, I am fairly sure that many "serious" investment professionals will discount the SWAG portfolio as somehow inappropriate or just lacking the type of financial complexity that typifies so many financial instruments. I have heard so many professionals tell me that gold isn't really an asset because it has no income stream. Likewise, I have had very good friends tell me that art has no objective "value" because it has no income stream and can only be valued by how much someone is prepared to pay for it. I am also used to hearing that assets such as art are highly volatile and do not really "fit" in a conventional portfolio. All of these criticisms appear to me as pure rubbish, and fail to understand the nature of the word "asset".

I will give my definition of an asset by means of a couple of examples. If I was in the jungle with a colleague and we heard from behind us some rustling and then suddenly out of the bushes came a tiger. In such circumstances, my ability to run faster than my colleague would most definitely be an asset to me. It has no income stream attached to it, but I am fairly certain that my colleague in the example would pay good money to have the asset. The asset has a potential value in a specific circumstance.

About two years ago, there was a tremendous flood at my house that washed my drive away. In over 20 years I have never claimed from my insurance company. But when the floods came, I made up for my earlier abstinence. The insurance company quite willingly paid a staggering amount to put right the extensive damage that had arisen from the flooding. Having house insurance is, most definitely an asset. Yet, it provides no income stream and quite often (in fact more often than not), it actually costs to maintain the insurance. However, when the time comes when you need to rely on that insurance, it was a great asset to have held. Assets do not need to provide an income stream. As flooding in my area has become more common, the insurance companies have recognised that the insurance that they provide has become more valuable, so it now costs more to keep this asset as the insurance premiums have risen. The next time an economist dismisses an asset's validity because it has no income stream, recognise him for what he is, naïve.

How is gold any different? Is it not insurance for the portfolio? As the risks against damage to the portfolio rise, so the cost of insurance should too. Gold acts as an insurance policy against portfolio storm damage. Why do so many economists refuse to see it as such? The inclusion of SWAGs in a portfolio provides a very useful diversification against many of the potential macro storms that will likely emerge. Over the last decade, such assets have already proven their ability to do this. With possibly another decade of portfolio storms to weather, serious consideration should be given to allocating a proportion of a portfolio to such assets.

The following chapters will take a look at each of the four SWAG categories and describe how they each perform a similar but crucial role in portfolio creation.

Summary Chapter 10

- SWAG assets are not just Silver, Wine, Art and Gold. SWAG is any asset that offers the owner some protection against money printing and financial repression (in whatever form that repression evolves).

- Governments have been in the business of financial repression (read expropriation) for thousands of years. The result has been that the rich have needed to evolve in order to preserve wealth.

- However, in this type of macro environment, it is not just the rich that need to protect their assets. All segments of society need to protect their assets, and that includes how portfolio and investment managers manage pension funds, insurance funds and endowment funds. It includes anyone with a self-managed pension and anyone with savings at all.

- The inclusion of SWAGs in a portfolio provides a very useful diversification against many of the potential macro storms that will likely emerge. Over the last decade, such assets have already proven their ability to do this. With possibly another decade of portfolio storms to weather, serious consideration should be given to allocating a proportion of a portfolio to such assets.

CHAPTER 11

Gold

Having worked in financial markets for the last 25 years, I can say that no specific asset arouses more passionate disagreement amongst financial professionals than gold. It is like the Marmite of the investment world. Gold has a spectrum of followers. To the far left of that spectrum are those that simply refuse to accept that gold is anything other than a decorative yellow metal that was once used as a form of money a long time ago. This group of thinking argues that gold is not now a financial asset and its value is a purely subjective issue. Further, this group would argue that gold has no place in the modern day portfolio. One further thing, this group of thinkers tend to be suspicious of the next group.

> Gold gets dug out of the ground in Africa, or someplace. Then we melt it down, dig another hole, bury it again and pay people to stand around guarding it. It has no utility. Anyone watching from Mars would be scratching their head.
>
> Warren Buffett

At the other end of the spectrum are those that believe that gold has always acted as a form of money and store of value. Further, that it has done so because it fulfils all of the criteria that economists suggest are necessary for that qualification as money. This group of thinkers have now also taken the argument forward to suggest that in a world of fiat currencies, gold now represents the ultimate hard currency. Rather than have a paper currency (with unlimited supply) that is supposed to represent a demand for a certain amount of gold, simply owning the gold is a purer form of money than paper money which quite often becomes worth less than it costs to print. This group of thinkers believe that gold acts as the most pure form of money, and that its performance within a portfolio creates diversification against other currencies as well as a form of insurance against sovereign default and rapid inflation. The two groups tend to dislike each other.

There is, of course, a third group of thinkers that have remarkably grown in number over the last decade. This group believes that economic catastrophe is in the process of unfolding and that our economic system will break down. This group has a fairly simple investment approach – gold and guns. As I hope has become clear, I am very much a part of the second group of thinkers. I believe that gold acts in two ways. Firstly it is the ultimate hard currency. Secondly, it acts as a form of house insurance for the rest of the portfolio.

As was demonstrated in Chapters 8 & 9, gold not only has the typical characteristics of traditional money but it also has other qualities that differentiate it. It is scarce and its supply is relatively fixed. Further, there is no associated debt with gold. Take any major currency and there is typically a high level of debt associated with that currency reflecting all the excess borrowing that respective governments have undertaken over the years. The following table shows a progression of various government debt profiles over the years, and includes a forecast for next year from the OECD.

Government debt % of GDP	1970	1990	2010	2012 (f)
Japan	11.1	63.9	198.4	210.2
USA	46.3	63.0	92.8	101.4
France	40.4	38.6	92.4	100.2
UK	69.5	32.3	81.3	94.5
Italy	55.2	97.6	131.3	133.0

If there was any single table of statistics that might win-over the gold sceptic, it should be the one above. To revisit George Classon's classic "The Richest Man in Babylon", a near fool-proof method for becoming rich is to consistently spend less than one earns. Yet, the above table shows governments throughout the last 40 years fairly consistently spending more than they earn. It is hardly surprising that creditworthiness has become an issue for sovereign states. When a government consistently spends more than it earns, and bridges the gap by borrowing more and more, eventually the problem of insolvency and bankruptcy emerge. If each of the above governments were private individuals, the banks lending to them would be urgently attempting to salvage the money they had lent and each individual would undoubtedly have very poor credit scores. It is no wonder that the credit rating agencies have the above economies under scrutiny.

However, there is one enormous difference between a government consistently over-spending and a private individual consistently over-spending, and that difference is the fact that if a government finds itself becoming insolvent, it can simply print more money to pay its debts. If a private individual did the same, they would be arrested for counterfeiting. Yet, since governments can print money at will, technically there should be no such thing as an outright default. Rather, the outcome from excessive money printing as a means of bailing out an over-spending government is a very weak exchange rate for the currency in question. If the Bank of England keeps printing more and more money to buy back UK government bonds, then the British Pound will eventually weaken.

It is in this guise that one needs to evaluate gold. Gold is often seen as a volatile commodity rather than a currency. However, any commodity exists in two states; it's normal state as a material that is useful for economic activity; and secondly as a currency - a store of value and a medium of exchange. Gold's use as a means of exchange dates back thousands of years. Indeed, gold coins are still in use today as a legal tender in many countries. Historically, many other types of commodities such as grains, fruit, timber and so on have acted as a form of currency.

This can apply to any commodity, but for reasons of durability and portability, the commodity which developed most successfully as a currency is gold. Indeed, gold derives significant value from its role as a quasi-currency - so, rather than supply and demand, gold's value is based on a relationship to the supply of other currencies, their relative <u>real</u> interest rates, and the assumed probability that gold moves beyond quasi-currency to become an actual currency that people need to hold. Once these points are accepted, gold becomes a commodity that can be evaluated against other currencies fairly simply.

An example may be useful. Oil has been one of the most fundamentally important commodities of the last century. Its discovery and use has led to rapid industrialisation and significant technological advances. But how much does a barrel of oil cost? This may seem like a trite question, but understanding the answer makes gold's role as a currency clearer. The following table looks at the price of a barrel of oil and an ounce of gold in USD terms. It also looks at how many barrels of oil an ounce of gold has bought.

So, back in 1900, an ounce of gold would have bought just over 42 barrels of oil. Over the next 100 years, that same ounce of gold saw its purchasing power fluctuate between being able to buy just less than 6 barrels of oil right up to 36 barrels of oil. Currently, an ounce of gold will buy just over 18 barrels of oil, which is above its average over the last 100 years of 16 barrels.

Year	Oil price,$/ barrel	Gold price,$ per ounce	Barrels of oil per ounce of gold	Barrels of oil per$
1900	0.45	18.96	42.1	2.2
1910	0.53	18.92	35.7	1.89
1920	3.50	20.68	5.9	0.29
1930	0.95	20.65	21.7	1.05
1940	1.02	33.85	33.2	0.98
1950	2.77	34.72	12.5	0.36
1960	2.91	35.27	12.1	0.34
1970	3.39	36.02	10.6	0.29
1975	12.21	160.86	13.2	0.08
1980	37.42	615	16.4	0.03
1985	26.92	317	11.8	0.04
1990	23.19	383.51	16.5	0.04
1995	16.75	383.79	22.9	0.06
2000	27.39	279.11	10.2	0.04
2005	50.04	444.74	8.9	0.02
2011 (est)	86.84	1600	18.4	0.01

Now, let's look at how well the US dollar has done. Back in 1900, one US dollar purchased just over two barrels of oil. Slowly, but surely, that purchasing power has been eroded and today the same US dollar will purchase just 0.01 (or 1%) of a barrel of oil. Since a barrel of oil is 159 litres, that implies that one dollar will buy just 1.6 litres of oil today compared with 353 litres in 1900. The fiat currency has lost over 99% of its buying power.

The credibility of a currency is based upon its ability to hold its purchasing power. Whether it is oil that is being purchased, real estate, food or any other good or service that composes a part of our standard of living, if a currency loses its buying power, one has to question whether its role as a currency is valid.

Based on the table above, it can be seen that the USD has lost over 99% of its purchasing power to buy oil. The next stage of the analysis here is to examine just how much money printing took place over the period examined. At the beginning of 1901, the US money supply measure, M2, stood at $10 billion. By August 2011, it had risen to at $9.5 trillion. Putting that into meaningful numbers, for every dollar that was around in 1901, there are now $957. From a graphical viewpoint, that looks something like this.

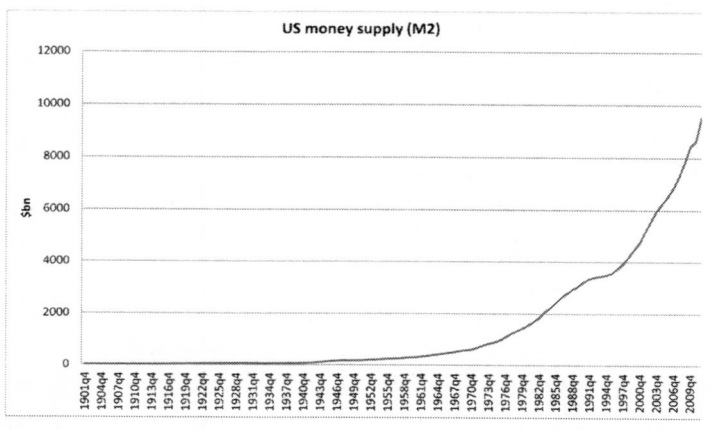

The real economy has grown by about *30* times since 1901, which implies that had the US money supply been allowed to grow in line with the real growth in GDP, then that initial $9.97bn would have (healthily) turned into around $300bn. The fact that reality shows it to have grown over 30 times more than that suggests, theoretically, that the purchasing power of the USD is likely to have fallen by around 97%. A rare confluence of economic theory and economic fact!

It seems fairly clear that over any meaningful period of time, the price of gold will reflect the relative supply of gold against the relative supply of a specific currency. Gold supply is relatively fixed in the short term (though one could argue its ultimate supply is definitely finite), whereas the printing of specific fiat currencies can vary widely. When a central bank decides to indulge in quantitative easing and expands the money supply of that currency aggressively, one should expect gold along with other currencies that are not being exposed to aggressive money printing to appreciate.

In a sense, the relative value of gold can be logically assessed by working out its P/E ratio. This would be its price divided by the global money supply. Dylan Grice, of Société Générale is the No. 1 Extel rated global strategist. Dylan has championed the idea that gold's value can be appraised logically. In his analysis, Dylan argues that the gold price would need to be around $10,000 per ounce for the US monetary base to be fully backed (i.e. $1 in existence for every $1 worth of gold). As Dylan admits, this may be an understatement since it takes the *global* stock of gold in existence but compares that with just the US monetary base. If one also included the printing efforts by other central banks, the price of gold would need to be higher.

What appears clear is that gold acts with two critical differences. First, thanks to the fact that governments have a long-established history of spending more than they earn, there is a very long history showing that such scenarios are inevitably accompanied by fairly liberal money printing. In the US example above, the money supply M2 was expanded at an annual average rate of almost 6.5% for over 100 years. Fiat currencies tend to see their respective money supplies expand quite liberally as and when a government gets into spending trouble. Governments throughout history get into such trouble. Unlike a fiat currency, gold supply is essentially fixed. Approximately 70% of all gold that exists has now been mined (c.165000 tonnes), so there is a finite amount of future gold supply that can come on stream too. This makes the supply side argument for gold very strong when compared with fiat currencies.

Gold's status as a "hard" currency is a very strong argument in its favour. Yet it also has another characteristic that differentiates it from fiat currencies. Namely, in times of crisis gold acts as a hedge against government. Agricultural land could be argued to offer a similar hedge against inflation as gold. Yet, at times of crisis, you can't pack your agricultural land into a bag and move. Land can be taxed and even confiscated. Gold, thanks to its portability, then, acts as an insurance policy against government-induced economic crises.

I started work In August 1987 as a fresh-faced trainee Economist at Greenwell Montagu Gilt Edged. Within two months I was confronted with the October 1987 equity market crash. I was told that it was a once-in-a-lifetime experience. That was, of course, until the next crisis came along. It took me about 10 years to realise it, but the fact of the matter is that pretty much every year sees some once-in-a-lifetime crisis. After a while I realised that I was making a career from anticipating them. Whilst most of the economic fraternity were busy using their mean-regression econometric models to predict trend GDP in 1-2 years' time, I was busy looking at the factors that would prompt the next economic crisis. Where would it happen? When would it happen? One was bound to happen somewhere, so the correct analysis was to assume that and therefore have eyes open for that. Crises come thick and fast. The list is just a taster and is by no means complete.

1987 – Global equity market crash

1988-90 – US savings and loans crisis

1988 – Norwegian banking crisis

1989 – Argentinian currency crisis

1990-92 – ERM crisis

1991 – Finnish and Swedish banking crisis

1992 – Mexican, Finnish and Swedish banking crisis

1993 – Venezuelan banking crisis

1994 – Mexican and Turkish currency crisis

1995 – Argentinian banking crisis

1994-96 – Brazilian banking crisis

1997-98 – Widespread Asian currency crisis

1998 – Russian financial crisis

2000-01 – Turkish currency crisis

2001 – 9/11 Twin Tower attack

2001-2 – US dot.com crisis

2007-2009 – US credit and banking crisis

2010-11 – European sovereign debt crisis

Over the course of the last century, literally hundreds of different currency crises have taken place. Professor Graciella Kaminsky's 1999 study entitled "The Twin Crises: The Causes of Banking and Balance-of-Payments Problems" studied 20 different economies between 1970-1995 finding 26 different episodes of banking crises and 76 different episodes of currency crises. One of the commonalities cited behind the crises was a prior debt-fuelled economic binge.

Considerable research has subsequently been undertaken in an attempt to understand how and why currency crises recur so regularly. In 2010, Professors Reinhart and Rogoff undertook an exhaustive study of financial crises over the last eight centuries in their book "This Time it is Different". Reinhart and Rogoff introduce their book in the following way:

If there is one common theme to the vast range of crises we consider in this book, it is that excessive debt accumulation, whether it be by the government, banks, corporations, or consumers, often poses greater systemic risks than it seems during a boom. Infusions of cash can make a government look like it is providing greater growth to its economy than it really is. Private sector borrowing binges can inflate housing and stock prices far beyond their long-run sustainable levels, and make banks seem more stable and profitable than they really are. Such large-scale debt build-ups pose risks because they make an economy vulnerable to crises of confidence, particularly when debt is short term and needs to be constantly refinanced. Debt-fuelled booms all too often provide false affirmation of a government's policies, a financial institution's ability to make outsized profits, or a country's standard of living. Most of these booms end badly.

Reinhart and Rogoff added to their research on the subject with their 2010 paper entitled "Growth in a Time of Debt." Their concluding remarks state the following:

The sharp run-up in public sector debt will likely prove one of the most enduring legacies of the 2007-2009 financial crises in the United States and elsewhere. We examine the experience of 44 countries spanning up to two centuries of data on central government debt, inflation and growth. Our main finding is that across both advanced countries and

> emerging markets, high debt/GDP levels (90% and
> above) are associated with notably lower growth
> outcomes.

I appreciate that I have quoted that text before. But, if
something is worth saying, it is worth saying twice. As
a reminder, the OECD predicts that the US government
debt/GDP ratio will hit 101% next year. Other notable
expectations are 101% for Portugal, 210% for Japan,
133% for Italy, 142% for Greece, 100% for France and
116% for Ireland. The average government debt/GDP
ratio across the entire OECD is predicted to rise to
103%. If Reinhart and Rogoff have got their sums
right, it suggests that economic growth in the OECD is
going to be very sluggish for a prolonged period of time.

This makes perfect intuitive sense. Extremely high levels
of borrowing imply that governments need to tax more
and have much less room to spend freely. Indeed, once
borrowing becomes too extreme, then economic growth
can clearly stagnate quite sharply. Japan's government
debt ratio rose to over 90% in 1996. Between 1986 and
1996, Japanese GDP grew by an average of 3.2% per
annum. Since 1996, however, GDP growth has averaged
just 1.2% per annum. Now, I appreciate that die-hard
Keynesians will simply argue that had the Japanese not
run enormous budget deficits, then GDP post-1996
would have been even weaker. The beauty with their
critique is that one can never disprove it. However, what
can be said is that Japan certainly fits into the Reinhart
and Rogoff theory and it certainly makes perfect sense
that high levels of debt impede growth, in the same way
that an excessively high mortgage debt would impede a

household's ability to spend on discretionary items. Reinhart and Rogoff's 90% theory is, what I consider, a defining point for gold. It is a tipping point that makes gold ownership not only sensible but imperative.

This 90%-debt paradigm creates what many call an "unsustainable debt dynamic." Looked at in simplistic terms, an unsustainable debt dynamic occurs when the numerator in the equation (level of debt) is growing faster than the denominator (nominal GDP). Hence the debt/GDP ratio is constantly growing. If the ability for the economy to grow is impaired by the high level of debt, then this becomes a vicious circle resulting in an ever-upwards spiralling of debt that eventually has just one possible outcome: default. This is repeat analysis, but crucial to the rationale for gold ownership.

I think it is fair to say that economic crises do happen all the time. However, the crisis that is currently unfolding has a uniquely different texture to it. In many of the examples from my crisis list above, the problems derive from a country-specific problem. Maybe the Mexicans borrowed too much. Maybe the Swedes attempted to keep their currency pegged at a highly uncompetitive rate. Each had its own fabric.

The current position is somewhat different insofar as the problem of excess borrowing seems to have become endemic across a very wide spectrum of not only banks and financial institutions across the world, but also sovereign states. In an environment where a sovereign default risk in a country like Greece or Portugal runs the risk of creating a major global financial collapse, the price of insurance becomes extremely valuable. This is a relatively unique situation. Academic study after academic study has shown how a specific economy can get into severe economic trouble when it over-borrows, but what happens when most of the OECD economies have over-borrowed and are in a debt trap?

There is no revelation in the idea that rising indebtedness creates a higher risk of default. Yet, in an environment where many governments appear to have entered an unsustainable debt dynamic, the obvious question about gold so rarely gets asked. Can gold go bust? The answer is that it can't because there is no associated debt attached to gold. It sounds such a trite point to make, but it is actually crucial. The US dollar, Euro, Pound or whatever fiat currency one cares to mention carries with it an associated amount of government debt. Once that government debt becomes so high that the only way out is through money printing, the risk of either an outright default or debasement through a substantially weakened exchange rate becomes real. Gold has no debt associated with it. It can't go bust. It can't be debased. It can't be infinitely supplied. Gold provides one of the very few hedges against government in such a predicament.

Quality assets gravitate to strong hands

It is interesting to look at who has been buying gold as this provides insights. In September 1989, at the annual meeting of the IMF, the 11 central banks constituting the ECB along with Sweden, Switzerland and the UK signed an agreement that would limit their sales of gold to no more than 400 tonnes annually over the coming five years. Even since this agreement was signed, the advanced economies of the world have, generally speaking, been net sellers of gold.

What has become more and more clear, however, is that the emerging economies have started to become net buyers of gold. It is as if the weak hands are passing their good assets to the strong hands. Quality assets gravitate to strong hands.

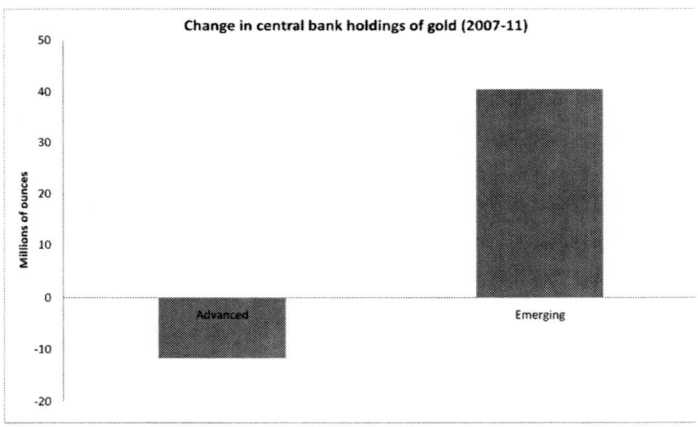

Over the first 8 months of 2011, emerging economy central banks added significantly to their physical holdings of gold, with Mexico, Russia, Thailand and Korea being major contributors.

The above graph refers specifically to central bank holdings of gold. If one excluded central banks and looked instead at household ownership of gold, demand falls into two categories; jewellery and investment use. Generally speaking, Chinese households have been the driving force in gold demand over the last few years. In 2011q3, Chinese households bought 200 tonnes of gold representing almost one quarter of global consumer demand. Chinese demand has virtually doubled over the last 4 years. Over the same period, household demand from the US and Japan (combined) has fallen from 58 tonnes to 54 tonnes.

European interest in gold is interesting. As the fear of a break-up in the Euro has intensified, the demand for gold has altered dramatically. Over the last year (to 2011q3), the most dramatic increase in household demand for gold has come from Swiss and German households. The following graph plots the changes in ownership over the last year.

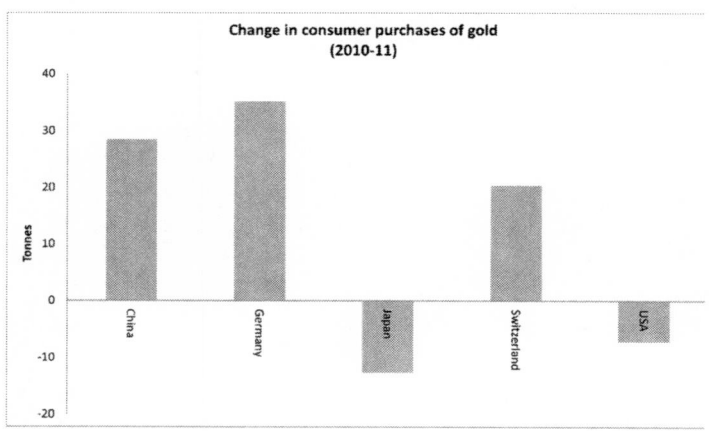

The trend for disinvestment within the US and Japan continues, and the trend for accumulation in China continues. Germany and Switzerland, however, become major net buyers. One cannot help but reason that the fear of a Euro debacle plays a big part in this.

A number of trends emerge. Emerging central banks tend to be net buyers of gold. Advanced central banks tend to be small net sellers. Within the household sector, the US and Japan have seen persistent small net selling, whereas Chinese households have been the driving force behind the buying. Over the last year, the fear of Euro-implosion has led to Swiss and German households raising their demand for gold significantly.

These are all trends. They are covered by one central theme; weak hands are selling gold to strong hands.

Chapter 11 Summary

- When a government consistently spends more than it earns, and bridges the gap by borrowing more and more, eventually the problem of insolvency and bankruptcy emerge. However, there is one enormous difference between a government consistently over-spending and a private individual consistently over-spending, and that difference is the fact that if a government finds itself becoming insolvent, it can simply print more money to pay its debts.

- Considerable research has been undertaken in an attempt to understand how and why currency crises recur so regularly. In 2010, Professors Reinhart and Rogoff undertook an exhaustive study of financial crises over the last eight centuries. The truth of the matter is that currency crises happen all the time and reckless government borrowing is more often than not the cause. As a reminder, the OECD predicts that the US government debt/GDP ratio will hit 101% next year. Other notable expectations are 101% for Portugal, 210% for Japan, 133% for Italy, 142% for Greece, 100% for France and 116% for Ireland. The average government debt/GDP ratio across the entire OECD is predicted to rise to 103%.

- There is no revelation in the idea that rising indebtedness creates a higher risk of default. Yet, in an environment where many governments appear to have entered an unsustainable debt dynamic, the obvious question about gold so rarely gets asked. Can gold go bust? The answer is that it can't because there is no associated debt attached to gold. It sounds such a trite point to make, but it is actually crucial. The US dollar, Euro, Pound or whatever fiat currency one cares to mention carries with it an associated amount of government debt. Once that government debt becomes so high that the only way out is through money printing, the risk of either an outright default or debasement through a substantially weakened exchange rate becomes real. Gold has no debt associated with it. It can't go bust. It can't be debased. It can't be infinitely supplied. Gold provides one of the very few hedges against government in such a predicament.

- Gold has also proven its ability as a general store of value. Back in 1900, an ounce of gold would have bought just over 42 barrels of oil. Over the next 100 years, that same ounce of gold saw its purchasing power fluctuate between being able to buy just under 9 barrels of oil right up to 36 barrels of oil. Currently, an ounce of gold will buy just over 18 barrels of oil, which is above its average over the last 100 years of 16 barrels. Now, let's look at how well the US dollar has done. Back in 1900, one US dollar purchased just over two barrels of oil. Slowly, but surely, that purchasing power has been eroded and today the same US dollar will purchase just 0.01 (or 1%) of a barrel of oil. The credibility of a currency is based upon its ability to hold its purchasing power. Whether it is oil that is being purchased, real estate, food or any other good or service that composes a part of our standard of living, if a currency loses its buying power, one has to question whether its role as a currency is valid.

- It seems fairly clear that over any meaningful period of time, the price of gold will reflect the relative supply of gold against the relative supply of a specific currency. Gold supply is relatively fixed in the short term (though one could argue its ultimate supply is definitely finite), whereas the printing of specific fiat currencies can vary widely. When a central bank decides to indulge in quantitative easing and expands the money supply of that currency aggressively, one should expect gold along with other currencies that are not being exposed to aggressive money printing to appreciate.

- Quality assets gravitate to strong hands. Emerging economy central banks have been accumulating gold while advanced economies have been net sellers. Demand from Chinese households has been one of the major drivers of global demand in recent years. Quality assets find their rightful home.

CHAPTER 12

Silver

Many of the reasons that apply to owning gold also apply to silver. Indeed, in many areas there is an identical rationale. However, applying a similar analysis to silver as was applied to gold suggests that silver has not done as good a job at preserving purchasing power as gold. Back in 1900, an ounce of silver cost $0.62c. Had that kept pace with the rise in money supply, one might reasonably have expected silver to be trading at $60 or more today. It has certainly provided some insulation against the ravages of money printing, but has not been perfect. It should also be taken into account that silver supply has also risen.

Having said that, the inclusion of silver in SWAG as well as gold was done deliberately because going forward, silver can be expected to have a distinctly different persona to gold since silver is not just a poor man's gold. It has unique characteristics that make its inclusion in SWAG important. Indeed, one of the purposes for including silver is to capture secular changes that are taking place across the world, changes that play directly to many of silver's strengths. For example, the call for cleaner sources of energy and heating as well as health care issues on sanitation and cleaner water. All of these issues have a direct bearing for silver.

Before the advent of digital cameras, the use of silver halide and silver nitrate in film development was responsible for around 30% of the consumption of silver. When the photographic market shifted away from the use of standard film development to digital cameras, it was believed that silver demand would collapse. Demand from photography did, indeed, collapse. At the turn of the century, the photography market used some 250m ounces or more per year. By 2011, the annual demand from the photographic industry is expected to be closer to 100m ounces. Yet, despite this collapse in demand from photography, the overall demand for silver has tended to rise courtesy of the significant rise in demand from other new and growing industrial areas.

Around the turn of the last century, industrial demand for silver represented 30% of total demand. Industrial demand is defined here as total demand excluding demand from photography and jewellery. It would include demand from areas of industry such as electronics and batteries, photovoltaic panels and superconductors. According to the CPM Group's silver survey for 2011, industrial demand now accounts for 54% of the demand for silver. That increase from 30% to 54% is a dramatic change in demand structure within a ten year period.

Silver has a number of physical qualities that is leading to its industrial demand rising sharply. Silver has the highest conductivity of any metal. It also has the highest reflectivity too. This, coupled with its strength and durability, is turning silver into an industrial metal with a great deal of potential usages.

Perhaps the most startling new use for silver has been in the field of solar panelling. It takes about 80 tonnes of silver to produce a Giga Watt (GW) of electricity. In 2000, there was essentially no demand for silver for solar panelling. Today, it is estimated that approximately 13 GW of electricity are produced via solar panels. Future demand looks set to rise even faster.

To get some idea of how much future demand could come from this area of industry, one need only look at the planning in place across different economies. China has announced plans to increase its solar energy capacity from around 5 GW at present to 20GW by 2020. By 2020, India plans to increase its capacity from essentially scratch to 20 GW (and 100GW by 2030). The US plans to increase its capacity from around 5GW at present to 20 GW by 2020. If one conservatively pencils-in another 20-40 GW for the rest of the OECD and emerging markets then we can expect to see photovoltaic demand rise from around 13GW at present up to perhaps 100GW over the next decade. This is a conservative estimate. There are several forecasts looking for global generating capacity to rise by as much as 40 times the current level over the coming decade.

VM Group's Jessica Cross gave a presentation to the London Bullion Market Association in November 2009 that assumed a more conservative estimate, and factored in a 10-15% per annum increase in demand from this sector over the coming decade. Of course, there will always be analysts who argue that science will develop a cheaper way of using solar panelling without silver. Anything "might" happen. Non-silver coating thin film panels will possibly take market share. Silver loading efficiencies will likely improve. Cross takes both of such risks into account in making her forecast. Yet, even her conservative estimate sees a trebling in demand by 2020.

In my view, the potential demand that appears set to come from electricity production from solar panelling should not be underplayed. It could easily represent 20-30% of total silver demand within a decade. But solar panelling is not the only area offering growth in future demand for silver. Considerable academic research has now been conducted into the use of silver as a means of enhancing food hygiene and water purification. Thanks to the fact that silver ions prevent bacteria and algae build-up, silver is fast replacing many of the harsher chemicals that have traditionally been used for such purposes (such as chlorine and bromine). Silver ions prevent Legionnaire's disease and their use in hospitals is becoming more and more common.

Silver's use in medicine, however, is not a recent phenomenon. Cyrus, the King of Persia (550 BC) was recorded to have had his water drawn from a steam, boiled, and then carried around in silver vessels by donkeys following him wherever he went. Pliny the Elder recorded in 78 AD that silver had healing properties as an ingredient in bandages, being extremely effective in healing wounds. According to the Silver Institute, the ancient Phoenicians knew that water kept in silver vessels stayed fresh during long sea voyages.

Yet, despite its long history, it is really only recently that silver's use in medicine has started to accelerate. The reason for this is that scientists have only recently understood *why* silver has the unique medical properties that it has. In medical terms, there are three mechanisms through which silver manages to prevent bacteria spreading; catalytic oxidation of cell surface radicals to inhibit transfer of oxygen, reaction with surface radicals on the surface of the bacteria and viruses to interfere with electron transport, and binding with DNA in disease organisms to prevent unwinding. These are the medical formats. In simple language, silver basically kills the bacteria! As the Silver Institute describes it:

> Quite simply, silver interrupts a bacteria cell's ability to form chemical bonds essential to its survival. These bonds produce the cell's physical structure so bacteria in the presence of silver literally fall apart. Cells in humans and other animals have thick walls and are not disturbed by silver. Therefore, silver prevents bacteria growth but is harmless to humans.

Silver usage in medicine, however, is really only just starting. Trials are on-going using silver-impregnated materials as a protection against the MRSA superbug. MRSA is a bacterium that can live harmlessly on the skin of healthy people but can lead to serious infection if it enters the blood stream. MRSA is resistant to almost all chemical antibiotics; so many hospitals are employing silver-imbedded equipment including surgical tools, catheters, needles, stethoscopes, furniture, door handles and even paper files. The following is a typical report on the subject from the Sunday Times in November 2009:

> Tiny particles of silver are to become the latest weapon in the fight against the MRSA superbug in Scottish hospitals.
>
> Giltech, an Ayr-based technology company, is to start clinical trials on products it hopes to roll out across every NHS trust in Scotland. Its hair and body wash and nasal ointment, containing silver ions, will be used on infected patients in hospitals run by NHS Ayrshire & Arran. The aim is to eliminate the spread of the bacteria, which can be fatal.
>
> Gillian Watson, the chief executive, believes the technology would be effective on almost any bacteria, including C. difficile. She said: "Silver is nature's own anti-microbial. It essentially smothers the bugs so they can't breed, eat or reproduce. With existing products which are mainly alcohol-based, they kill the bugs that are there, but as soon as you touch your nose or a patient, they can re-colonise. With this, the ions remain and give you ongoing protection.
>
> "Silver kills all bugs. We have lists of hundreds of thousands of pathogens and microbes that it will be effective against." Ions are put into a special glass called Arglaes, created by Giltech. The shower gel contains small pieces of the glass, which dissolves on contact with liquid, releasing the ions onto the patient's skin.

Trapping the ions in the glass means Giltech can measure exactly how much silver is used, keeping it within recommended levels of exposure. Watson said: "We can adapt our technology to be put into products for different applications. This technology could be incorporated into almost everything a hospital could use."

It is not the first time silver has been used to prevent infection: the Romans and Greeks used the metal to keep water supplies clean, and it was used as an antibacterial agent by surgeons in the First World War.

In the UK, it is estimated that 300,000 people develop a healthcare-associated infection such as MRSA each year, killing about 5,000 patients.

Although the potential for silver demand to rise from such uses is not, perhaps, as startling as the prospects from solar panelling, it is still nonetheless likely to be secular in nature. Water purification, food hygiene, fibre and textile usage, wound care and medical use all represent major sources of future demand for silver.

According to the ABN Amro "The Silver Book" (July 2011), industrial demand for silver is expected to rise from just over 50% of identifiable demand up to 70% over the next decade. The following table was kindly put together with the assistance of the VM Group, the same provider of data that was used for the ABN AMRO report. According to this data, demand for uses of silver can be expected to follow the following path.

Tonnes (demand)	2000	2002	2004	2006	2008	2010	2011e	2015f	2020f
Batteries	464	483	503	505	589	657	756	1344	2010
Mirrors	430	448	467	485	515	584	701	1542	1822
Water purification	325	449	622	726	846	898	942	1145	1462
Solar panels	36	50	109	234	603	568	628	1013	1960
Food hygiene	5	15	25	39	61	88	132	534	648
Radio frequency tags	0	2	8	14	34	65	118	210	367
Fibre/Textiles	0	0	0	0	50	47	52	153	214
Medical applications	10	15	25	39	61	76	90	381	631
Total	1270	1462	1759	2042	2759	2983	3419	6322	9114

Between 2000 and 2011, the industrial uses of silver rose by an average 9.4% p.a. The assumptions embedded for the forecast out to 2020 assumes an average growth of 11.5% p.a. for the coming years. Given that many of these uses are relatively new technologies, it is plausible that demand growth proves an upside-surprise to these estimates.

The arguments supporting future demand for silver are, generally speaking, not particularly contested. One can debate about how conservative these estimates are, but even the more conservative forecasters suggest that the new-use growth outlook is very impressive.

Those arguing against the metal will point out that large amounts of silver eventually gets re-cycled and becomes available as future supply. Long-term bears of silver have typically argued that the ability to recycle silver once it has been used is one of the biggest drawbacks for the metal from an investment perspective. It is, then, pertinent to highlight the fact that the growth in new uses of silver will generate very little recycling as it will not be commercially viable to collect. The ABN AMRO report summary puts it clearly:

> The silver supply-demand balance will continue to show signs of structural improvement and start to become much tighter than it has for decades. For new uses, the amount of silver actually used in each product is comparatively minute, but volume growth potential is huge. This sector will eventually offset the demand slack left by the shrinking use of silver in the photographic industry. Moreover the volumes of

scrap silver generated by these new applications will be exceptionally small as it will not be commercially viable to collect and recover the scrap metal.

The impact of higher prices will have a trivial impact on demand, and there is little evidence that a material shift towards substitution has begun in the majority of demand applications. Both substitution and thrifting of the metal are expected to be minimal, due to silver's unique physical properties. We will therefore see a level of demand that will be price inelastic over the next decade.

The future supply of silver is taken as a given. There are plenty of mines that produce silver and, generally speaking, silver production tends to increase each year. The following table is taken from the Silver Institute:

Supply (millions of ounces)	2004	2005	2006	2007	2008	2009	2010
Mine production	613.0	637.3	641.7	665.4	681.9	718.3	735.9
Net government sales	61.9	65.9	78.5	42.5	28.9	15.5	44.8
Silver scrap	195.2	198.6	203.3	199.0	193.7	188.4	215.0
Producer hedging	9.6	27.6	-	-	-	-	61.1
Total supply	879.7	929.5	923.5	907.0	904.5	922.2	1056.8

As can be seen from the table, mine production has edged up throughout the last decade. On average, it has risen by just over 2% per annum. It is assumed that as new demand arises, supply will be readily available. There are two reasons why this may not be so simple. First, most silver mining occurs as a by-product. Typically, silver is a by-product from gold mining or copper mining. Hence, it is the demand for copper and gold that impacts how much silver gets mined. Silver production from mining rarely reacts to price movements in silver itself making the supply curve from mining very inelastic. If price for silver doubles, it is very difficult for mining companies to generate production of anything more than the 2-3% that has been typical of the last decade.

Second, it is commonly assumed that there are limitless amounts of silver in the ground. Estimates of unexplored silver will always be imprecise. However, according to the US Geological Society the potential volume of silver left to be mined is extremely low. Using a study by Professors Reller and Graedel, the prospects for many metals have been projected based on current levels of consumption. The following article is taken from the "New Scientist" from May 2007:

> The calculations are crude - they don't take into account any increase in demand due to new technologies, and also assume that current production equals consumption. Yet even based on these assumptions, they point to some alarming conclusions. Without more recycling, antimony, which is used

to make flame retardant materials, will run out in 15 years, silver in 10 and indium in under five. In a more sophisticated analysis, Reller has included the effects of new technologies, and projects how many years we have left for some key metals. He estimates that zinc could be used up by 2037, both indium and hafnium - which is increasingly important in computer chips - could be gone by 2017, and terbium - used to make the green phosphors in fluorescent light bulbs - could run out before 2012. It all puts our present rate of consumption into frightening perspective.

If full-scale monetary debasement became the prognosis, gold would rise substantially. Silver, too, would see very sharp rises in price. Silver and gold share the same type of SWAG characteristics in this respect. However, silver's inclusion in SWAG was not solely due to its hard currency status. That role can easily be filled by gold. Rather, silver's inclusion is because not only does it have hard currency characteristics but it also has future demand characteristics that could underpin a sharp rise in its price regardless of any potential money-printing. The new industrial uses for silver have the potential to transform silver as an industrial metal and for that reason silver has a clear role to play as a SWAG.

Summary Chapter 12

- The inclusion of silver in SWAG as well as gold was done deliberately because, going forward, silver can be expected to have a distinctly different persona to gold. Indeed, one of the purposes for including silver is to capture secular changes that are taking place across the world, changes that play directly to the potential for silver's importance as an industrial metal to rise.

- Despite the collapse in demand for silver from photography, the overall demand for silver has tended to rise courtesy of a significant rise in demand from other new and growing industrial areas. Around the turn of the century, industrial demand for silver represented about one-third of total demand. According to the CPM Group's silver survey for 2011, industrial demand now accounts for 54% of the demand for silver. That increase from 30% to 54% is a dramatic change in demand structure within a ten year period. According to the ABN Amro "The Silver Book" released in July 2011, industrial demand for silver is expected to rise to 70% over the next decade. Silver is being transformed into a major industrial metal.

- Perhaps the most startling new use for silver has been in the field of solar panelling. In 2000, there was essentially no demand for silver for solar panelling. Demand started to pick up in 2005. Thereafter, demand has become exponentially stronger. Technologies can always change, but future solar panel demand looks set to make silver usage in industry even more significant.

- Considerable academic research has now been conducted into the use of silver as a means of enhancing food hygiene and water purification. Thanks to the fact that silver ions prevent bacteria and algae build-up, silver is fast replacing many of the harsher chemicals that have traditionally been used for such purposes (such as chlorine and bromine). Silver ions prevent Legionnaire's disease and their use in hospitals is becoming more and more common. Yet, despite its long history, it is really only recently that silver's use in medicine has started to accelerate. The reason for this is that scientists have only recently understood why silver has the unique medical properties that it has.

- Mine production has edged up throughout the last decade. On average, it has risen by just over 2% per annum. It is assumed that as new demand arises, supply will be readily available. There are two reasons why this may not be so simple. First, most silver occurs as a by-product. Typically, silver is a by-product from gold mining or copper mining. Hence, it is the demand for copper and gold that impacts how much silver gets mined. Silver production from mining rarely reacts to price movements in silver itself making the supply curve from mining very inelastic.

- Second, it is commonly assumed that there are limitless amounts of silver in the ground. Estimates of unexplored silver will always be imprecise. However, according to the US Geological Society, the potential volume of silver left to be mined is extremely low. Using a study by Professors Reller and Graedel, based on current levels of consumption, many metals (including silver) have a very restricted limit of supply. Indeed, given that silver's use in many of the new technologies renders it near impossible to recycle, the supply curve for silver appears set to be very inelastic. As price rises, supply will not be able to respond.

CHAPTER 13

Wine

Is investing in wine a good idea? The Liv-ex index of the top 100 'investment grade' wines has increased by about 250% over the last decade. Indeed, wine has tended to appreciate at a time when many traditional assets have struggled.

As with any investment, an indiscriminating approach might well result in disappointment. The adage 'caveat emptor' does indeed apply, especially to older wines. But empirical studies show that the addition of fine wine to a portfolio of investments can simultaneously boost returns and reduce both risk and skew in a portfolio.

In periods of 'risk aversion' in financial markets, financial assets tend to become more correlated and diversification strategies tend to become less effective. However, a recent empirical study published by Masset and Weisskopf (Raise Your Glass: Wine Investment and the Financial Crisis), covering over 400,000 data points between 1996 and 2009, shows that fine wine tends to have a conspicuously low correlation with other financial assets, especially during periods of financial crisis.

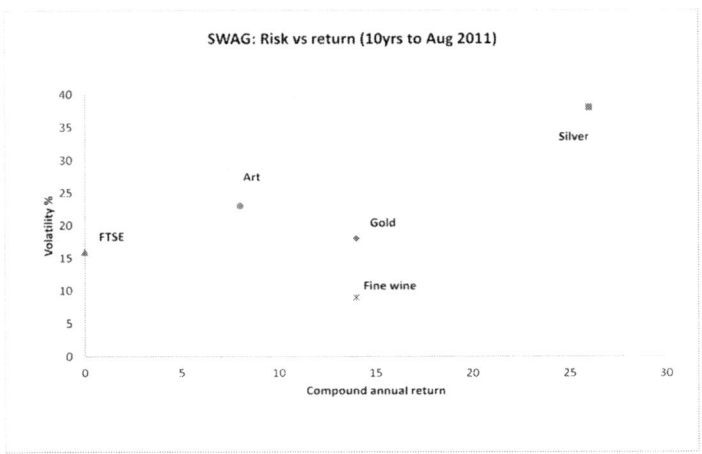

In the chart above, fine wine prices over the 10 years to August 2011 provided an annual return of just below 15% per annum with a volatility of just below 10%. The FTSE 100 provided a return of close to zero with a volatility of around 15%. Gold had a similar level of volatility to equities, but provided a return close to wine. Silver is on its own producing a mouth-watering return of around 25% per annum but with volatility of close to 40%. Art sits with a return of around 7-8% but with a volatility of just over 20%.

Specifically, fine wine's defensive characteristics were particularly pronounced and impressive in the equity market meltdowns of 2000-03 and 2007-09. In the first episode, the S&P index declined by about 45% peak-to-trough while the fine wine index (FWI) rose by about 4%. In the second period the S&P declined by over 50% while the fine wine index fell by 13%; but it only took the FWI ten months to recoup those losses. At the time of writing the equity market was still materially below its

2007 peak. It is this ability to add value to a portfolio via diversification that signals wine as a valuable SWAG.

As previously stated, academic research agrees. Masset and Weisskopf conclude:

Our results show that since 1996, the General Wine Index and particularly first growth wines from top vintages have performed better than equities while showing a lower volatility.

A further and more detailed research into different investor types and wine indices fully supports the evidence and confirms that wine in a portfolio has produced higher returns and lower risks than the Russell 3000 equity index during the period of time. Especially in times of economic downturns such as in the periods 2001-03 or 2007-09 the defensive characteristics of wine are most pronounced. Wine's performance has declined less than other assets. It had an even lower volatility (with one exception) and also showed improved skewness and kurtosis measures. Fine wines may therefore be regarded as an interesting addition to an investor's portfolio.

Perhaps more than any SWAG asset the supply of fine wine is finite in that as each and every bottle of a particular fine wine is consumed its supply goes down. As an extreme example the now legendary Northern Rhone wine Jaboulet Hermitage La Chapelle 1961 was released for ten French francs, or less than one pound, a bottle. Now a single bottle will fetch nearly 10,000 pounds. There are not many bottles left!

Moreover, for tax purposes wine is considered to be a 'wasting asset' (a useful life of less than 50 years) and hence is not subject to capital gains or income tax. A carefully researched and calibrated approach to wine investing should therefore pay dividends in the long run, particularly now that, as explained in earlier chapters, fiat money regimes have entered a more dangerous phase.

By way of background, more than 99% of wine is better thought of as a consumption good than an investment good. These days most wine is bought in supermarkets; it is meant to be drunk as young as possible and is usually consumed within 24 hours of purchase. To qualify as an investable asset a wine must at least have the capacity to age - preferably in a predictable fashion. This usually requires a track record from previous vintages.

Blue chip investment grade wines, like many other commodities, are in a secular bull market for essentially the same reason: to accommodate the huge increase in demand as rapidly growing emerging markets like China compete for the scarce supply of the most desirable wines.

In the case of wine this tendency is reinforced by two powerful forces. Firstly, the increasingly skewed distribution of wealth and incomes and the rapidly swelling ranks of the super-rich, especially in emerging markets, which tends to push up the prices of the trophy wines relative to the merely outstanding ones. Secondly, and related to the first point (see discussion in earlier chapters) the inevitability of more debt monetisation, which benefits the wealthy and those 'in the know' first, as the major OECD countries are faced with the dilemma of choosing between this and the even more frightening option of debt deflation.

First let's explore some of the arguments for and against investing in wine in more detail.

The case against wine as an investment asset and counterarguments:

- Argument #1: Relative to some other SWAG assets wine is not always easily portable; it can go off and it can be variable. A given wine from a given vintage is not always homogeneous; even bottles from the same case can vary. Moreover, bottle variation tends to increase with age, hence the adage there are only good bottles not good wines. Therefore wine is arguably not a reliable store of value.

- Counter-argument: Typically wines in an investment portfolio will never come out of storage or have not been released from bonded warehouses, so portability is rarely an issue. The wines can be bought and sold 'in bond.' Ownership can shift without incurring a tax liability and without the product being physically moved. Usually investment grade wines are purchased at a young age, often on release, and given that they are typically stored in sealed wooden cases in climate-controlled environments, bottle variability is not usually a problem.

- Argument #2: Storage and insurance costs can be significant. Moreover wine is not a particularly 'liquid' investment in that there is usually a considerable wedge between its liquidation value and its replacement value.

- Counter-argument: To be a viable investment a wine should be valuable enough from the outset for the storage and insurance charges not to matter. A storage charge of £15 a year is material for a case of wine costing £150, but not really for a case costing £1500 or more. It is also fair to say that all investments carry costs of one form or another. Further, there is a significant difference between liquidating a physical cellar typically consisting of opened cases and odd bottles in less than ideal storage conditions and liquidating a professionally managed portfolio of investment grade wines in a bonded warehouse. The prices of good quality, non-trophy, wines have been rising steadily for sound fundamental reasons discussed in more detail below. Moreover over time the supply of any particular wine decreases as it is drunk, which tends to push up prices even if there are other imperfect substitutes (e.g., different vintages of the same wine).

- Argument #3: In America, interest in fine wine began to take off when Maryland lawyer-turned-wine critic Robert Parker arrived on the scene. After he correctly called the now legendary 1982 Bordeaux vintage, his status was elevated from expert to guru, and his rapidly swelling army of devoted followers hung on his every point score. Unwittingly he created a monster, which arguably distorted the wine market as prices became exponentially correlated to his scores. As prices of some 100 point wines have rocketed into the stratosphere there has been a bit of an anti-Parker backlash. If palate and liver fatigue eventually takes its toll, the end of the Parker phenomenon could unwind some of the irrational exuberance in the wine market.

- <u>Counter-argument:</u> While Parker has been instrumental in making wine more accessible to a wider audience in the early part of his career and has undoubtedly contributed to some market distortions, it is unlikely that the wine market would have evolved very differently without him. It is easy to overstate the influence of one individual. Arguably his influence has been on the wane for some time and this has not affected the wine market. If Parker were to disappear tomorrow it would make little difference.

- <u>Argument #4:</u> It is not unheard of - for example in Bordeaux - for wine prices to fall after their *'en primeur'* futures release either because chateau owners have been too optimistic about the prices their wines might command following previous successful campaigns, or because they are just plain greedy. Even if the price doesn't go down in the first few years after release the 'cost of carry' is considerable and your money is tied up. Moreover the problem with buying older wines is not just bottle variation but 'provenance' – you don't know where it has been.

- <u>Counter-argument:</u> This is where the skill and judgement of the professional investor comes in and there is no substitute for experience. For professional wine investing provenance is absolutely of the essence. Just like a portfolio of equities, a portfolio of wine requires skill and judgment in its composition. Academic research has shown that a portfolio of investment grade wines provides valuable diversification to a broad portfolio of assets.

Anatomy of the wine market: old world wines remain the most attractive investments

"Old world" wines are essentially represented by France, Germany, Italy, Spain and Portugal. Each of these countries produce some remarkably age-worthy wines: Port and Madeira for example can age for hundreds of years, while good German Rieslings, Italian Barolos, Spanish Rioja and wines from the major French regions can age over many decades. Ability to age is a necessary but not sufficient condition for investment: one also has to take into account how global tastes are evolving and how reliably wines age.

Aged Barolos (from Piedmont) and Brunello di Montalcino (from Tuscany) can be spectacular but do not have a track record of ageing reliably. Uncorking a 40-year old Barolo or Brunello is a lottery. So-called Super-Tuscans, which burst on the scene in the 1970s, show a lot more promise in this regard. Modern techniques suggest this should become progressively less problematic for younger Italian wines, but it will take time for a track record to be established. Port, on the other hand does age reliably well, but suffers from being relatively unpopular and prices have been static in comparison with many other regions. Global tastes appear to be shifting inexorably away from sweet, fortified wines to dry table wines. That could change but appears unlikely on any foreseeable horizon. However given the price to quality ratio (QPR) a small allocation to Port would be worth having.

German Riesling, on the other hand, having been out of fashion for some time, does appear to be making a comeback, deservedly so because it can age beautifully and arguably offers outstanding value for money. Good German Riesling is generally a much better investment proposition than white burgundy, which in recent years has been blighted by premature oxidation (aka 'premox'), which affects the wines randomly and unpredictably even in individual cases. In spite of this burgundy is still regarded as the source of the greatest dry white wines in the world. However, this has not always been the case. At the beginning of the 20th century the most celebrated and expensive white wines on restaurant lists were German Rieslings. On a QPR basis, Rieslings also seem to deserve a small allocation.

Red burgundy thankfully appears to be unaffected by the scourge of premox and appears to have shed its image of unreliability, which existed up until about a decade ago. Moreover, some of the most exhilarating red wines in the world come from burgundy, while output of the top estates is but a small fraction of that of many of the most celebrated Bordeaux chateaux. This would seem a sure-fire recipe for strong investment returns. The only drawback with red burgundy is that it can evolve in an unpredictable way. For example it can be precocious in its youth and then shut down hard for an unknown number of years, during which the wine sometimes provides very little drinking pleasure and can even appear to be flawed - drawbacks for a consumer, but not necessarily for an investor. Red burgundies should form a key part of the wine portfolio.

Unlike Burgundy, Bordeaux tends to age in a beautifully linear and predictable fashion. In fact Bordeaux is *the* wine investment *par excellence*. In good vintages top Bordeaux tends to improve steadily for 20-30 years before reaching its plateau of maturity, which typically will last for many years. Whereas one often frets over when exactly to drink other – for example Australian - wines and catching them before they go over the hill or literally hit the wall, this is rarely if ever a problem with well stored Bordeaux. This applies to dry red and white Bordeaux and sauternes, arguably the greatest sweet wine money can buy, which like Port is also somewhat out of vogue.

In Bordeaux the quality of winemaking has come on in leaps and bounds. In the 20th century there were several legendary Bordeaux vintages, for example 1929, 1945, 1947, 1953, 1959, 1961, 1982, 1986, 1989, 1990 and 1996, but there were also far too many duds particularly in the 1960s and 1970s. These days, outstanding wines are made even in the most difficult growing conditions given much greater attention to detail and the march of technology. The great modern vintages – 2000, 2005, 2009 and 2010 - will probably eclipse the most celebrated 20th century vintages. Even some of the less heralded vintages like 1998, 2001, 2002 and 2006 have produced some notably age-worthy wines, which will be stunning when they reach their plateau. Bordeaux, then, is a necessary and central part of any wine portfolio.

Wine's evolution in an historical context

It is unlikely that wine is just a passing fad. After all, wine has biblical connections. In Greek mythology it was referred to as the 'Juice of the Gods' and Dionysus was the god of wine, later to become known as Bacchus in Roman times. In fact the history of wine is inextricably intertwined with the history of human civilisation itself. Don't believe anyone who tells you that Parker 'discovered' Rhone wines. It was the Greeks and the Romans.

However, in Britain, it was barely more than a generation ago that fine wine was largely the preserve of the aristocracy, while the masses were condemned to drinking supermarket plonk. The Australians changed all that in the 1980s when, taking advantage of a weak Australian dollar and employing savvy marketing, they shipped over decent affordable wines, which were not unpleasant to drink. They were hardly investment grade, but they did open the door to many future wine consumers who subsequently changed their drinking habits over the years.

Since then wine has gone in two directions. The bulk of wine now sold in supermarkets is commoditized, anonymous and anodyne, and produced by large conglomerates. In the other direction are more esoteric wines produced by generally smaller, fastidious estates, always striving to push the quality envelope. So in some sense there are no bad wines any more as in the 1970s, only interesting ones and boring ones. It is the more esoteric wines that have piqued the interest of wine consumers and potential wine investors.

Almost certainly there has been a permanent change in tastes in favour of wine over the last couple of decades. In economics jargon the demand curve has shifted (to the right) so that for a given price more wine will be consumed. The health benefits of drinking wine continue to accumulate: modest consumption (especially of red wine) increases longevity, reduces the risk of heart attack, strokes and cancer and is associated with a lower incidence of obesity and brain degradation with age.

The Lafite phenomenon

The most important development in the wine market in the last decade or so has been the spread of interest in fine wine from traditional European and North American markets to other countries including the BRICs. In China the demand for blue chip investment grade wines has soared to the point where the UK- and US-based auction houses achieve most of their turnover in Hong Kong. As these emerging economies industrialise further, a growing middle class will likely accelerate the spread of wine drinking culture more and more.

The Lafite phenomenon has been truly staggering with the price of certain vintages of Chateau Lafite having gone up nearly tenfold over the last decade. Lafite, or "La Fei" as it is called, has become the number one status symbol in China. The brand has become popular because it is associated with success. Loosely interpreted La Fei means 'on the up' and on the path to riches. The price of Lafite has left every other Bordeaux first growth trailing in its wake.

What has been even more spectacular and even more bizarre is the Carruades phenomenon. Carruades de Lafite is the 'second wine' of Chateau Lafite. It is produced at the same estate but is a very different animal to the 'Grand Vin' and while pleasant it is clearly an inferior wine. In the 1990s it cost less than 15 pounds a bottle. However, those slightly less well-heeled Chinese have been piling into Carruades to the point where its prices has risen approximately twenty fold. Carraudes, which crazily in some vintages has become more expensive than some other first growths like Chateau Haut Brion, is a clear example of what can happen when an asset with fixed supply gets swamped by demand.

From around the middle of 2011 the price of Lafite started to correct lower. Clearly this has potentially further to go especially if the world economy weakens and China slows down in sympathy. Would it be reasonable to expect the price of Lafite to unwind much? It seems unlikely because the demand eventually will be there and the quality is second to none. Sure we may have seen an overshoot in Lafite but the much bigger story is a permanent increase in the equilibrium price. For fine wine in general the biggest story is the huge structural shift in the demand curve, which barring a global ice age is likely to be permanent in nature. It is this interaction between supply and demand that makes Lafite (as well as most investment grade wine) very interesting from an investment perspective.

The price of wines like Chateau Lafite is unlikely to crash for many reasons, three key and related ones among them: First, the demand curve for Lafite has shifted substantially and permanently to the right and there is much more 'brand recognition' now than ever before. Lafite is not just a phenomenon it is a legend. Second, this brand recognition is most visible among the super-rich and new money elites that can afford to buy it by the case load. Third, the quality of the product has never been higher. Over the centuries there have been some legendary Lafites, but they are all eventually likely to be eclipsed by the best of the most recent vintages. This is generally true of other first growth Bordeaux as well. So, clearly, demand for investment grade wine has shifted significantly. For many assets, such a development typically attracts new suppliers and new supply comes on stream preventing a marked shift up in prices. But with investment grade wines like Lafite, supply is almost perfectly inelastic. It does not really matter how rapidly demand grows, only so many bottles of Lafite can be produced in any given year. Indeed, for historical vintages, with each bottle consumed, the supply curve actually shifts to drive prices even higher. As every student of economics knows, when a demand curve shifts to the right and a supply curve shifts to the left, price gets driven sharply higher.

As explained in earlier chapters more quantitative easing and debt monetisation is inevitable. The immediate trickle down tends to benefit the richest first. The price of Lafite and other first growth Bordeaux may correct but this will represent a buying opportunity as the money printing process evolves.

In summary, the key story in wine is the shift in preferences towards fine wine – in other words a substantial and permanent increase in demand. While this will elicit some supply response the new equilibrium price is likely to be much higher than the initial equilibrium. Fine wine supply will remain finite, particularly as it is consumed. Moreover empirical studies show that fine wine can boost investment returns of a portfolio whilst reducing risk and skew. Fine wine has particularly good defensive qualities during economic crises - in more ways than one.

Summary Chapter 13

- Empirical studies show that addition of fine wine to a portfolio of investments can simultaneously boost returns and reduce both risk and skew in a portfolio. In periods of 'risk aversion' in financial markets, financial assets tend to become more correlated and diversification strategies tend to become less effective. However, a recent empirical study published by Masset and Weisskopf covering over 400,000 data points between 1996 and 2009, shows that fine wine tends to have a conspicuously low correlation with other financial assets, and especially during periods of financial crisis. Specifically, fine wines defensive characteristics were particularly pronounced and impressive in the equity market meltdowns of 2001-03 and 2007-09.

- Perhaps more than any SWAG asset the supply of fine wine is finite in that as each and every bottle of a particular fine wine is consumed its supply goes down. As an extreme example the now legendary Northern Rhone wine Jaboulet Hermitage La Chapelle 1961 was released for ten French francs, or less than one pound, a bottle. Now a single bottle will fetch nearly 10,000 pounds. There are not many bottles left!

- Almost certainly there has been a permanent change in tastes in favour of wine over the last couple of decades. In economics jargon the demand curve has shifted (to the right) so that for a given price more wine will be consumed. The health benefits of drinking wine continue to accumulate: modest consumption (especially of red wine) increases longevity, reduces the risk of heart attack, strokes and cancer and is associated with a lower incidence of obesity and brain degradation with age.

- The most important development in the wine market in the last decade or so has been the spread of interest in fine wine from traditional European and North American markets to other countries including the 'BRICs.' In China the demand for blue chip investment grade wines has soared to the point where the UK- and US-based auction houses achieve most of their turnover in Hong Kong.

- The price of fine wines like Chateau Lafite is unlikely to crash for many reasons, three key and related ones among them: First, the demand curve has shifted substantially and permanently to the right and there is much more 'brand recognition' now than ever before. Second, this brand recognition is most visible among the super-rich and new money elites that can afford to buy it by the case load. Third, the quality of the product has never been higher. Over the centuries there have been some legendary Lafites, but they are all eventually likely to be eclipsed by the best of the most recent vintages. This is generally true of other first growth Bordeaux as well.

CHAPTER 14

Art

A Picasso on the wall? Well, that does the trick in a number of ways. It can be transported out of the country relatively easily should that be necessary. Since it produces no income, there is no income tax to be paid on it, or for that matter to alert the authorities of any wealth. It is in finite supply. Unlike many financial assets, a Picasso does not carry any incumbent debt. One doesn't have a mortgage on a Picasso and so foreclosure is not an issue. If the government decided to double the money supply, then the purchasing power of wages may well diminish, but in all likelihood, the price of the Picasso will simply just adjust upwards…possibly very rapidly since the money supply reaches Picasso buyers first!

I can just feel the hackles going up amongst the art connoisseurs of the world.

There is no question that art suffers when it comes to being seen as an investment. A very substantial majority of art collectors tend to frown at those who see works of art as something that could be evaluated materialistically, as a means of enhancing wealth. The number of times I have heard those connected with the art industry argue that an individual should buy a piece of art solely because of its aesthetic value to that specific individual is countless. Financial potential is one of those things that shouldn't be mentioned. It transgresses the line of art etiquette. Academic research even supports the idea that the average art investor is willing to give up some monetary return in exchange for its aesthetic pleasure (Goetzmann and Spiegel (1995)). I would go so far as to argue that a degree of snobbishness pervades the art market and that those who evaluate art according to its potential to generate financial return are seen as somewhat vulgar and totally missing the purpose and point of the art and its beauty. Art, it seems, has some ethereal mysticism. For some fun, I Googled "art quotes" and came up with the following;

The brilliance of art as a collectible is that it has a way of reaching out on an emotional level. It touches on mystery, even spirituality.

Buying art is the same thing as falling in love.

Cherished art becomes a portal through which we may enter the Universe... a glimpse, a sliver, a hint of our very own heaven. Artists are providing a personal journey to an emotional state of mind. Art is not a product, but a service.

It almost feels sinful to talk about art and money in the same sentence. As a result of this perception, art investment is not something that has taken off in the same way that, for example, wine investment has done. Whereas there are literally dozens of businesses set up to allow the average investor to invest in wine, the number of funds set up purely to trade in fine art for financial gain is relatively few. But it is certainly growing. My purpose here is not to get into the arguments of whether it is vulgar or not to use art as a means of wealth enhancement. My position on this issue is totally clear. I have absolutely no interest either way in whether or not it is vulgar. So long as it is legal, I want to evaluate it and determine if it should be a part of a portfolio. The evidence is quite conclusive.

Wine is a relatively easy asset to evaluate. One bottle of 2000 Chateau Lafite is, by and large, highly likely to be the same as another bottle. In effect, it is a commodity. That particular vintage of wine will be bought and sold on a daily basis by brokers and collectors throughout the world. Its price movements can be seen and are relatively transparent. A fine piece of art like Van Gogh's "Sunflowers", however, is unique. Tracking the price of it requires lengthy periods of inactivity between sales. Even with fine sculpture where editions of 10 or more allow more frequent instances for sales, it is not necessarily correct to treat one edition as identical to another. Often, the patina on an edition has aged in a nicer way that allows it to achieve a much higher price than exactly the same sculpture in the same auction. Art prices are much harder to measure.

But, again, that is not an excuse to ignore it. It is remarkable just how many academic studies have been conducted examining art as a financial asset. There have been literally dozens of studies examining art as a financial investment stemming from investment bank and broker research right through to full-scale rigorous academic studies. I am going to draw on the findings of a cross-section of these studies. Many of the studies address questions that are central to this book. I am really looking to answer one key question: is there a place for art inside a portfolio?

One of the most recent academic studies by Kraeussl and Lee (2010) entitled "Art as an Investment: the Top 500 Artists", looked at art as an investment over the last 24 years of data. The inference given in the abstract suggests that art tended to have a positive correlation with global equities but with a very high level of volatility and that it was not an interesting alternative asset to hedge returns of the global equity index. Such a conclusion, however, misses the point. Bananas are not a good alternative to apples, but their inclusion creates a more balanced diet. Art may not be an alternative to equities, but should they be included in a portfolio? Given Kraeussl's somewhat cold evaluation in the abstract of his report, it was a revelation to see his actual findings.

The following table shows the basic return and risk properties of a number of asset classes through the period of study (1985-2009).

	Quarterly return (%)	Standard deviation	Sharpe ratio	Jarque-Bera test	Skewness
Art	1.78	0.78	0.17	6403	5.7
Commodities	1.73	0.19	0.11	14.6	0.9
Hedge Funds	2.10	0.05	0.26	33.5	-0.8
Private Equity	0.00	0.14	-0.00	31.3	-0.2
Real Estate	1.57	0.12	0.09	6.9	-0.2
Global equities	1.12	0.09	0.03	13.2	-0.7
T-Bills	1.21	0.01	0.00	1.7	-0.1

The table is interesting from a number of angles. First, art as an asset class shows the second highest return over the 24 year period relative to the other 6 asset classes in the table. A quarterly return of 1.78% translates to an annualised rate of return of 7.3%. Kraeussl argues that it achieves such a high return only at the cost of a very high level of volatility. The standard deviation is indeed materially higher than the other asset classes. However, I think such a criticism misses a key point. The statistics on the Jarque-Bera test and the Skewness test reveal a vital characteristic of art. To quote the report:

> The Jarque-Bera test indicates that the returns on art are not normally distributed. Moreover, it has by far the most **positively** skewed distribution. Since the

distribution of the returns on art is right-skewed, extreme high returns on art are more probable than extreme low returns.

What does this mean in everyday language? It means that compared with other assets, art tends to be more volatile. It has more big moves than other assets on average. However, and this is the key point, those big moves tend to be up rather than down! That type of return profile is extremely attractive from an investment perspective.

Kraeussl went on to evaluate how art performs within an overall portfolio including nine different asset classes. The study recognises that investors vary in terms of their risk-aversion, so three different scenarios are created (low, average and high risk aversion). The study also runs different scenarios where a weighting constraint is imposed (no asset can be more than 15%). The study has many conclusions. But there are some major standout points. Regardless of how risk-averse an investor is, art is <u>always</u> a necessary component in an optimised portfolio. When the weights are allowed to fluctuate freely, the optimised portfolio for a risk-averse investor contains 4% in art. As risk-aversion falls, the proportion of art rises to 23% of a portfolio. The report concludes:

We conclude that, as the level of risk aversion rises, the amount that should be invested in art diminishes. However, in all cases art should be included in the optimal portfolio. Our empirical findings indicate that the top 500 artists in the world play a significant role in a well-diversified portfolio.

Kraeussl's analysis certainly provided very strong academic rationale for the inclusion of art in a portfolio. However, the positive skewness statistics that his study revealed deserved more attention. It is one thing for an asset to be seen as unattractive because it is very volatile, it is quite another when the bulk of that volatility always tends to be generated from explosive moves UP in price. It seemed odd to me that this characteristic did not receive more attention in the report. I would have thought that any asset class that managed to displace most other assets inside an optimised portfolio was a highly noteworthy observation. Dr. Rachel Campbell of Maastricht University conducted two studies that throw light on this.

Campbell's 2008 study, "Art as a Financial Investment" was similar to that of Kraeussl. Campbell conducts a very thorough research of the previous literature and provides a summary of the performance of art from that literature. The period of study covers some 400 years of data through 17 different studies! The first statistic that jumps out is that every single study covering all of the periods shows that art generates a positive real return. The range of real returns is 0.2% up to 8.3%. Obviously, the period studied will affect the real return significantly. The highest return looks at returns on just Picasso between the years of 1966–1994. The lowest return focused on just modern and contemporary paintings between 1983 and 1994. Each study will impart a certain bias. But the big picture is that every single study produced a positive real return. The average across all studies suggests a mean real return of 3.5%. In this sense, art gains significant credibility as an inflation hedge.

Campbell's database contained a mixed basket of 100 well-known artists from different segments of the art world and included sales data from over 109,000 auction sales covering the period 1980 to 2006. Not surprisingly, her results on performance were similar to Kraeussl, with the composite art basket giving an annualised return of 7.1% over the period. Campbell's portfolio allocation also revealed similar results, suggesting that against other asset classes, art outpunches equities, corporate bonds and commodities in terms of its usefulness as a diversifier in a portfolio. Campbell's numbers suggest a portfolio weight of between 2.8%-16% for art. The Kraeussl and Campbell studies provide very good cross-validation.

However, it is Campbell's 2005 study, "Art as an Alternative Asset Class" that really gets to the heart of the issue. What she does in this study is investigate how well art performs during different types of equity environment. Kraeussl argues that art has a positive overall correlation with equities rendering it as relatively undesirable as a hedge against equities. By examining the entire data period, Kraeussl may have missed a very key point. Namely, the overall performance may be positively correlated, but from an investors' point of view, the main interest will focus on how correlated art is during periods when equities are going down in price. It is during such periods that true diversification becomes very valuable.

In this sense, Campbell's results are very revealing. Almost 30 years of monthly data are used from 1976 to 2004, utilising data from over 800 auction houses and covering hundreds of different artists. The following table is taken from the study.

Monthly Returns % 1976-2004	All periods	Equity bear market* (5% worst months)	Equity bear market** (10% worst months)
Art	0.52%	+1.15%	+0.47%
Equity	0.85%	-9.53%	-7.22%

*this represents the 5% of months that have recorded the most extreme monthly falls in equity prices
**this represents the 10% of months that have recorded the most extreme monthly falls in equity prices

In times when equities are showing their most dramatic falls, art prices at auction are moving in the opposite direction and by a magnitude that is significantly above the average over the whole period. One can only speculate as to why this may be happening. Perhaps at times of sharp declines in equities, art represents a safe haven asset. One would expect government bonds to display a similar characteristic, providing positive returns in periods of sharp equity declines and negative returns during periods of equity euphoria. Well, at least in theory! The point here is that art is acting as a very significant hedge against equities during the periods when investors most need an asset to act as a diversifier. One of the many complaints that I have heard over the last few years from portfolio managers is that most assets have become highly correlated with each other and that during periods of high market stress, everything tends to fall. Well, to portfolio managers around the world, please read Dr Campbell's study.

Many portfolio managers recognise the need for diversification and will retort that commodities provide a decent diversifier in times of equity stress. Campbell investigates that subject too, and does indeed conclude that during periods of the sharpest equity falls, commodities produce positive returns. For the (5%) worst equity months, commodities produce a positive return of +2.2%. Given the relative liquidity of commodities, it is easy to see why they have gained acceptance within modern portfolio management. However, is it right to view commodities and art as offering the same diversification qualities against equities? Clearly, both produce positive returns during periods of sharp equity price falls. Yet, what happens during the periods when commodity prices are falling sharply?

Campbell performs a similar study looking at how well art prices perform during periods when commodities are suffering their most violent monthly declines. Her results show that during such periods of commodity price decline, art prices actually rise, and do so by an amount similar to their average monthly performance. In other words, art performs almost independently to commodities during periods of sharp commodity declines. Campbell concludes her study by arguing that:

> The protection offered by the art market during bear markets on global equities is highly beneficial, so a failure to invest, albeit a small fraction of the portfolio in art indices, would seem to result in inferior portfolio returns.

These respective studies by Campbell and Kraeussl fold together to provide extremely compelling arguments for investment in art. Nobody is trying to portray art as some form of investment panacea that covers all worlds without risk. Art is a volatile asset. Yet, the historical data suggests that this volatility comes from its numerous upside bursts in price rather than through just general volatility. Art tends to rise when equities are in sharp decline. Art tends to rise when commodities are in sharp decline. Under any set of circumstances, academic research shows that art *always* deserves at least some weighting in an optimised portfolio. That is a remarkable conclusion.

Each of the four SWAG assets potentially brings something different to the table. At no point do I believe that any of the SWAGs should dominate the weights in a portfolio. Yet, each in turn deserves a weighting. Art's role in the SWAG portfolio is very different to the other assets. It is assumed that equities will continue to represent the major portion of risk within a portfolio. In such circumstances, art provides a very useful diversifier.

Adriano Picinati di Tocello is a Senior Manager of Deloitte Luxembourg. He wrote a very entertaining article on why art should be considered an asset class. Tocello observes that recent trends that have been influencing fine art have been experienced within other groups of collectible assets such as fine wines, rare watches, precious stones or stamps. This observation certainly tallies with what one might expect in such collectibles given the theory behind SWAG. Tocello goes on to examine the factors that he believed to have been driving forces. He quotes Joseph Schumpeter who once observed that *"Queen Elisabeth owned silk stockings. [...] The capitalist achievement does not typically consist in providing more silk stockings for queens but in bringing them within reach of factory girls in return for steadily decreasing amounts of effort."*

Tocello goes on to define how this capitalism is positively impacting the art market:

- Art markets become more transparent due to research in finance and economics as well as data dissemination.

- As more and more countries are becoming wealthier, there are more artists and an increased interest in art from a larger community.

- The proportion of all luxury spending on art will continue to increase as investors look for assets that would retain their value in the longer term especially in a period of economic uncertainty.

- With an increasing population that holds increasing disposable income, it is only natural that there is an increase in demand. In 2003, Sotheby's biggest buyers came from 36 countries. Four years later, they were spread over 58 countries and their total number had tripled (The Economist, 2009).

- The supply of best works of art will always be limited and tends to appreciate over time. Especially for deceased top-artists as paintings are lost, or bought by museums and collectors.

- Art markets are more robust. According to Christie's CEO, Edward Bolman, the reduction of auction sales experienced at the end of 2008 and in 2009 was mainly not due to a reduction in demand but rather a reduction of supply.

- Around 80% of the auction transactions are estimated to be below EUR 10,000 which leaves the door open for many newcomers.

Such are the benefits from diversification that it would be worthwhile for small, medium and large private investors to investigate. There are certainly art funds available that offer low entry rates for investors. The rationale for larger pension fund and investment fund portfolios is very clear. The British Rail Pension fund was a pioneer in this respect, when it invested £40m (3% of its funds) in 1974 into fine art. The art was sold between 1987 and 1999 generating an annual compound return of 11.3%. Given that pension funds are supposedly meant to take a very long term view on their holdings, and given the diversification benefits, it would certainly seem logical for more institutional investors to devote some allocation to fine art. Art very clearly has a place in SWAG. Yet, institutional portfolio managers seem most reluctant to embrace it. One portfolio manager informed me that art was purely subjective and that it had no logical rationale behind it as an investment vehicle. History shows that art has performed stunningly well as an investment. Perhaps the institutional portfolio manager needs to be asked by his investors why he doesn't understand the value of art investment given its historical performance. Perhaps the inconsistency is with the portfolio manager who can ascribe logic to investment in companies like Enron but not to investment in Picasso.

Academic research has now framed the question for investors well. Art provides an extremely useful addition to a portfolio. Why don't more portfolio managers get involved to provide extra value to their clients?

Summary Chapter 14

- There have been dozens of studies examining art as a financial investment stemming from investment bank research right through to full-scale rigorous academic studies. One of the most recent academic studies by Kraeussl and Lee (2010) entitled "Art as an Investment: the Top 500 Artists", looked at art as an investment over the last 24 years of data. The study shows that art as an asset class has one of the higher returns over the 24 year period relative to the other major asset classes. A quarterly return of 1.78% translates to an annualised rate of return of 7.3%. Kraeussl argues that it achieves such a high return only at the cost of a very high level of volatility. Art has more big moves than other assets on average. However, and this is the key point, <u>those big moves tend to be up rather than down.</u> That type of return profile is extremely attractive from an investment perspective. I am all against volatility in an asset unless that volatility is constant upside surprises!

- Kraeussl went on to evaluate how art performs within an overall portfolio including nine different asset classes. Regardless of how risk-averse an investor is, art is <u>always</u> a necessary component in an optimised portfolio. A stunning conclusion.

- Maastricht University's Rachel Campbell's 2008 study, "Art as a Financial Investment" was similar to that of Kraeussl. Campbell's literature review provides a summary of the performance of art over

some 400 years of data (through 17 different studies).
Every single study covering all of the periods shows
that art generates a positive real return. The range of
real returns is 0.2% up to 8.3%.

- However, it is Campbell's 2005 study, "Art as an
Alternative Asset Class" that really gets to the heart
of the issue. What she does in this study is investigate
how well art performs during different types of equity
environment. According to Campbell, in times when
equities are showing their most dramatic falls, art
prices at auction are moving in the opposite direction
and by a magnitude that is significantly above the
average over the whole period. Art is acting as a
significant hedge against equities during the periods
when investors most need an asset to act as a
diversifier.

- Many portfolio managers recognise the need for
diversification and will retort that commodities
provide decent diversification in times of equity
stress. Campbell investigates that subject too, and
does indeed conclude that during periods of the
sharpest equity falls, commodities produce positive
returns. However, is it right to view commodities and
art as offering the same diversification qualities
against equities? Both produce positive returns
during periods of sharp equity price falls. Yet, what
happens during the periods when commodity prices
are falling sharply?

- Campbell shows that during such periods of sharp
commodity price decline, art prices actually rise, and
do so by an amount similar to their average monthly

performance. In other words, art performs almost independently to commodities during periods of sharp commodity declines.

- These studies by Campbell and Kraeussl fold together to provide extremely compelling arguments for investment in art. Academic research shows that art always deserves at least some weighting in an optimised portfolio.

CHAPTER 15

Supply and Demand:
the Mexican Standoff

A strange standoff exists between investors who appear to understand the rationale behind investing in physical assets and those that do not. There are extremely bright individuals on both sides. Yet, when two extremely bright individuals take a diametrically opposite view of the same set of facts, it creates a great deal of friction and worry. Those that don't see the logic have concerns that they are missing something important. Those that do see the logic seem puzzled that others do not see the same logic. The first party pick up on that puzzlement which makes them even more paranoid about missing something big. The continual and often comical battle between the two groups rages on. Warren Buffett is one of the most outspoken anti-gold proponents. His musings on the subject are widely quoted:

> Gold is a way of going long on fear, and it has been a pretty good way of going long on fear from time to time. But you really have to hope people become more afraid in a year or two years than they are now.

And if they become more afraid you make money, if they become less afraid you lose money, but the gold itself doesn't produce anything.

I will say this about gold. If you took all the gold in the world, it would roughly make a cube 67 feet on a side…Now for that same cube of gold, it would be worth at today's market prices about $7 trillion dollars – that's probably about a third of the value of all the stocks in the United States…For $7 trillion dollars…you could have all the farmland in the United States, you could have about seven Exxon Mobils, and you could have a trillion dollars of walking-around money…And if you offered me the choice of looking at some 67 foot cube of gold and looking at it all day, and you know me touching it and fondling it occasionally…Call me crazy, but I'll take the farmland and the Exxon Mobils. Oct 2010

At the time of this latter comment, of course, Buffett was correct to say that gold would have purchased what it did. But of course, back in October 2010, gold was trading at $1340 an ounce. At today's prices it would buy quite considerably more than Buffett's analogy suggests. At today's prices one could throw in McDonalds, Starbucks, and some (well most) of the banks too.

The underlying point that Buffett makes, however, probably goes to the heart of why so many investment professionals disagree on metals like gold and silver. Their focus on supply rather than demand is skewed.

Buffett, effectively, highlights the fact that whatever gold has ever been mined still exists. Whether it is above or below the ground, it still exists. The same is not quite as true for silver as some silver gets depleted through degradation and unrecoverable usage. But, by and large, it is a fair point to argue that the supply of silver and gold is substantial when one takes into account the amounts below the ground yet to be mined and the amounts above the ground that sit as potential supply.

The supply in any year will equal how much new metal is mined plus how much old metal is "scrapped". The bearish view taken is that this above-ground supply is potentially enormous.

I think this way of thinking of supply is misleading for a number of reasons. If one collected all the US dollar bills in supply and put them into an enormous warehouse, it would represent Buffett's big block of gold. Like gold, the US dollar bills would need to be guarded. Like gold, the intrinsic value of the paper money serves no special purpose. And like gold, the paper money can be exchanged for real physical assets and companies. Why does Buffett criticise gold rather than the alternative fiat money? The total supply of gold has a fixed size warehouse in which it can be stored. The ability for global central banks to expand the money supply is essentially limitless. A potentially limitless number of warehouses would be needed to store the paper money. Anecdotes of wheelbarrows of money being needed to buy loaves of bread during the hyper-inflation of the Weimar Republic in Germany give some insight into the fallacy of potential supply. Why is it not legitimate to criticise paper money in the same way Buffett criticises gold?

Let us assume that both bulls and bears of silver and gold can agree that the above and below ground stores of gold and silver have always been around the same amount. The supply is finite. Whether it is above or below, the potential supply is fixed and finite. Most will agree on this.

Demand, however, is not fixed. Demand is linked to the money supply and is essentially limitless. As the money supply expands, so too does nominal GDP. Over the course of the 20th century, US money supply M2 expanded by over 1000 times it's starting point. So the asset used to purchase gold or silver is expanding rapidly, while the supply of the asset being purchased is totally fixed. The result is that the fixed supply assets will always cost an increasing amount of the expanding supply asset to buy. The more dollars they print, the more expensive gold will become.

When the bears talk about supply of physical assets, they should really be focusing on the supply of unlimited fiat money in relation to the supply of those physical assets. There is a finite amount of gold and silver. Picasso is no longer painting new work. Chateau Lafite 1996 is no longer being produced. These are all assets with a finite physical supply. When assets with a fixed supply become scarce relative to a potentially unlimited supply of money, and when those with that money "need" to acquire the assets, a potentially explosive move in prices occurs.

There is nothing particularly new in that thinking. But what is new is a potential situation where, possibly for the first time in history, in order to industrialise to the same standard of living as the OECD economies, the emerging economies will need more physical commodities than actually exist. This will result in a competition for such scarce assets and a rationing brought about by higher and higher prices. It is very plausible that this BRIC industrialisation process is creating a whole new supply problem for the world. Just as the world thought that a barrel of oil in 1970 was quite expensive at $3.39, it was soon to find that oil at $12.21 in 1975 was also not expensive. Nor was it expensive at $37.42 in 1980. At the time, it was seen as a bubble. Today, $37 per barrel looks dirt cheap. Oil is a special case perhaps, but a supply constraint on metals will act in exactly the same way. Where Chateau Lafite 1996 was once seen as *cheap* at £70 a bottle, it is now seen as cheap at £900 a bottle.

The Mexican stand-off is one of misunderstanding. The bulls of physical assets are looking at how many warehouses would be needed to house the physical assets in relation to how many warehouses would be needed to house the supply of fiat money. The bears are looking at the above-ground physical assets in relation to the yet-to-be mined physical assets and seeing that the former is large in relation to the latter, implying plentiful supply. Mr Buffett, how many warehouses would be needed to house the supply of global money? As Warren Buffett states, gold itself does not produce anything. But neither, Mr Buffett, do pieces of printed paper money. They both represent a means of exchange. Which would you rather have as a means of exchange? That is the right question to address.

Summary Chapter 15

- A strange standoff exists between those who claim to see the logic behind investment in physical assets like gold and silver and those that still see it as illogical and without intellectual foundation.

- The bear market view of gold and silver often takes the standpoint that if the amount of above-ground supply was taken into account then the supply of gold and silver would be enormous. Scrapping is indeed a major source of silver supply already. The bears seem fixated on this potential for above-ground supply to come on stream.

- Evaluating supply as a relationship between above-ground and below-ground resources, however, is almost certainly the wrong focus. The supply-demand issue that needs to be evaluated is the ratio of fiat money to the physical asset. How many warehouses would be needed to house all the silver that exists on this earth? Probably quite a few. But how many warehouses would be needed to house all the money that has been printed? That would be substantially more. As governments print more and more fiat currency, its supply rises faster than that of the physical asset like gold or silver.

- Indeed, given that it is a truism that the total supply of gold or silver must be finite (unless we start importing from another planet), then the price of the metals should theoretically be a function of just how much fiat currency is printed. One can always argue that other assets represent "better" investments, but it is hard to argue that the physical assets like gold and silver should not ALWAYS appreciate against an expanding fiat currency base over time.

- As Warren Buffett states, gold itself does not produce anything. But neither, Mr Buffett, do pieces of printed paper money. They both represent a means of exchange. Which would you rather have as a means of exchange? That is the right question to address.

CHAPTER 16

New Demand; Billionaire Boys and their Toys

Rothbard's seminal analysis on money-printing highlighted the fact that Austrian economics had found a flaw in the traditional classicist monetary thinking by pointing out that when the money supply gets expanded, it impacts different segments of society in different ways. For some it is tremendously positive. When those that it affects so positively can affect (in a significant way) the price of specific assets, it is worth taking the time to understand the process. The following is snapshot taken from an article in the Financial Times from September 2011.

> Two things make Christian Levett stand out: most strikingly, the 41-year-old set up the world's largest commodity hedge fund, the London-based Clive Capital, in 2007. The other intriguing aspect is his collection of about 700 antiquities, one of the largest in private hands. This smorgasbord of ancient Roman, Greek and Egyptian treasures was unveiled in June at Levett's new Museum of Classical Art in Mougins, a

hilltop chocolate-box French village nestled between Cannes and Grasse.

But Levett is not just obsessed with antiquities. Dotted around the displays are 60 classically inspired pieces by blue-chip modern and contemporary artists such as Marc Chagall, Paul Cézanne, Alexander Calder, Andy Warhol, Roy Lichtenstein and Henri Matisse. Some juxtapositions are more successful than others: Yves Klein's "Vénus Bleue" (1982) deftly dovetails with a first-century marble torso of Venus, but Damien Hirst's paint-splattered resin skull ("Happy Head", 2007) jars with a Roman bronze head of Apollo.

According to Forbes, in 2008 Levett made $130m. He "started to go ballistic", buying up to 25 per cent of works at key auctions from the collection of the late antique weaponry specialist Axel Guttmann.

This is a classic example of a wealthy and financially sophisticated individual deciding that a good way of storing his wealth is through works of art. What happens when the wealth of such buyers rises? The marginal propensity to spend on assets is almost 100%. Then, given the limited supply of Chagall and Cézanne, prices can become very strong. In reality, two factors are taking place. First, the level of global wealth is rising very sharply. Second, the concentration of that wealth is being allocated to a new breed of super-rich. This is creating a new demand curve for SWAG assets. A new demand paradigm.

A decade ago, the net worth of the world's richest 50 people was a staggering $600bn. Today, the richest 50 billionaires have a combined worth of just under $1.2tr. While equity markets have been virtually static, the concentration of wealth into the hands of the rich has been moving at pace. According to official statistics, total world wealth in 2000 amounted to $113tr. By 2010, total world wealth had risen to $195tr. So, it is quite clear that despite all the problems in financial markets and economies over the last decade, global wealth has been rising sharply.

If one looks at the composition of the richest billionaires, a decade ago approximately half of the richest 100 billionaires were American, whereas only 5% came from the BRIC economies. Today, some 32% are American and some 33% are from the BRIC economies. So, not only is global wealth rising, but it is being driven by a new breed of billionaire. The statistics are replicated across countries. A decade ago, the US accounted for 35% of global wealth. Today, it accounts for 31%. A decade ago, China accounted for 4% of global wealth whereas today it accounts for 8.5%. Similar stories can be seen for other emerging economies. India has seen its share of global wealth almost double from 1.0% to 1.8%, in Russia from 0.2% to 0.6% and Brazil from 0.8% to 1.7%. The BRIC global wealth share has risen from 6.1% to 12.6% over the decade.

A mix of three different factors is taking place. Global net wealth is rising. The share of that wealth owned by the super-rich is rising. The proportion of that super-rich group is becoming more diverse, with emerging economy BRIC representative accounting for a much higher number. If there had been the same increase in global wealth but it had been spread uniformly across the world, this would not have created the same demand dynamic that provides the fuel for SWAG assets. It is because global wealth is developing in the way that it is, that demand becomes focused laser-like on the type of assets that the super-rich buy. SWAGs.

The result is a massive pool of potential buying power for SWAGs. Unlike the more mature billionaire dynasties, the driving force behind the growth in global wealth is relatively new money that needs to start protecting the new-found wealth in the same tried and tested way that all wealth gets protected. The statistics do support the argument. Over the last decade, China and India have seen a massive accumulation of non-financial wealth. In terms of wealth per adult, the World excluding China & India has seen a rise of 15% in the accumulation of non-financial assets from $10,400 per head to $11,938. China & India, however, have seen a rise of 173% from $5077 per head to $13,865.

As the wealth filters down from the super-rich to the rich to the middle classes, the demand for SWAG assets will be broadened. How much of an impact could there be? Well, the statistics on wine consumption are very revealing. Somewhat amusingly, the Vatican City has the highest wine consumption per capita in the world at 70 litres per head. France and Italy take up proud top 10 positions with consumption of 45 litres and 42 litres respectively. Russia has some way to go at just 8 litres per head, but China is a mere novice at just 1 litre per head.

The potential for wine consumption growth to rise across the BRICs as wealth cascades through the economy is clear.

The same effect is being felt in the art world. It seems that it is always a surprise when a piece of art fetches a new record price. If one Google's "record art prices", the internet will unfold an enormous time-line showing new record after new record. The following is an article that appeared in Tate Magazine on 24th September 2011, bang in the middle of a fairly major equity market downturn and European credit crisis.

Christie's art auction on Tuesday has proved that the art world is not short of cash. In New York, works from French Impressionists Monet and Rodin were sold at record prices.

The art world can take heart. A Monet and a Rodin pulled in record prices at a Christie's auction on Tuesday, putting aside fears for now that the global credit crunch would crush prices.

The auction of Impressionist and Modern Art reaped 277 million dollars. The highlight: Monet's painting of a railroad bridge from his early period. "Le Pont du Chemin de fer a Argenteuil" sold for $41.5 million, topping the previous high for a Monet by nearly $5 million.

The hammer shattered records for Giacometti's bronze sculpture of a standing woman. It pulled $27 million, nine million more than the previous record. And the Rodin sculpture called "Eve" went for $19 million, more than double the previous record.

Christopher Burge, the Christie's Auctioneer: "Generally speaking, for the very best things, the market was still red hot and top prices were more than we expected."

If one puts the best Monet ever auctioned in a room with 10 multi-billionaire art collectors, the chances are that they might be less price sensitive than bidders of lower wealth. To a billionaire, owning the best of an asset class is important. In discussing art prices with Christie's, I was told that the strongest part of the market is at the very top end where the richest billionaires compete with each other for the very best assets. It is a little bit like the size of boats in Monaco harbour. For the super-rich billionaire who owns the biggest boat in the harbour, it is not acceptable to see a competing billionaire with a bigger boat. The old boat will be sold and a new even bigger yacht ordered. With essentially unlimited buying power, the super-rich will attempt to acquire the very best assets within an asset class. In economic terms, the demand for such assets becomes price inelastic, meaning demand does not fall much at all even when price rises. This effect, however, eventually filters down through the wealth chain.

The Credit Suisse Global Wealth report for 2011 contains a new and interesting section where it attempts to project future changes in household wealth. In 2011, they estimate total global household wealth at $231 trillion. They project that number to rise to $345 trillion by 2016. However, it is the composition of that increase that is particularly interesting. The report predicts that China will add a total of $18 trillion to the stock of global wealth over the next 5 years, replacing Japan as the second wealthiest country in the world. The following is taken from the 2011 report:

> Over the next five years, we expect to see a big improvement in the position of the emerging economies. Wealth in both China and Africa as a whole is projected to rise by 90%, but India and Brazil are forecast to do even better, with personal wealth more than doubling by 2016

The following table uses data from the Credit Suisse 2011 Global Wealth Report. It shows the number of millionaires recorded and how this is expected to change by 2016.

Number of millionaires (000's)	2011 actual data	2016 forecast	% increase 2011-2016
Brazil	319	815	155%
Russia	95	171	80%
India	204	510	150%
China	1017	2381	134%
BRICs	1635	3877	137%
World ex BRICs	28039	42703	52%

As the table demonstrates, the growth in the number of super-rich is highly concentrated in the emerging economies. Excluding the BRIC economies, the number of millionaires in the rest of the world is growing at about 8.8% per annum. In the BRIC economies, the number of millionaires is growing at 19% per annum. BRICs are the new millionaire machines. Given the significant boost in global money printing over the last few decades, is it any surprise that the number of rich and super-rich have grown in number so dramatically? When that money printing combines with the industrialisation of a number of large emerging economies, the confluence of events provides a sweet-spot for demand growth. When that sweet-spot for demand happens to coincide with a relatively unusual tightening in supply, then new paradigms occur for specific assets. It is a rare mixture of events all happening at a similar time. It is no wonder the price movements of some assets have been bewildering.

Summary Chapter 16

- Previous chapters have examined in detail the broader macro-arguments for SWAG assets. There are, however, some very powerful micro-arguments that are also having a big impact.

- A mix of three different factors is taking place. 1) Global net wealth is rising. 2) The share of that wealth owned by the super-rich is rising. 3) The proportion of that super-rich group is becoming more diverse, with emerging economy BRIC representative accounting for a much higher number.

- The Credit Suisse Global Wealth (CSGW) report for 2011 contains a new and interesting section where it attempts to project future changes in household wealth. In 2011, they estimate total global household wealth at $231 trillion. They project that number to rise to $345 trillion by 2016.

- The composition of that increase in global household wealth is particularly interesting. The CSGW report predicts that China will add a total of $18 trillion to the stock of global wealth over the next 5 years, replacing Japan as the second wealthiest country in the world.

- If one looks at the composition of the richest billionaires, a decade ago approximately half of the richest 100 billionaires were American, whereas only 5% came from the BRIC economies. Today, some 32% are American and some 33% are from the BRIC economies

- If there had been the same increase in global wealth but it had been spread uniformly across the world, this would not have created the same demand dynamic that provides the fuel for SWAG assets. It is because global wealth is developing in the way that it is, that demand becomes focused laser-like on the type of assets that the super-rich buy. SWAGs.

- The result is a massive pool of potential buying power for SWAGs. A new demand paradigm.

CHAPTER 17

What if the Economic Outlook is Different?

The economic background against which SWAG theory is based presumes that the debt default dynamic is almost unstoppable and that governments will inevitably resort to the tried and trusted method of money printing to "solve" the problem. One can argue that a number of alternative economic outcomes could be possible. The money printing scenario that I take as my central case is not the only possible outcome, though I believe clearly that it is the most likely. Economics, however, is always about a balance of probability, and other different economic outcomes are possible. It is worth outlining some of these different economic outcomes in order to assess how SWAG would perform should a different economic path evolve.

Everything turns out just fine – the Goldilocks scenario

If the money printing was withdrawn, what chances of a recovery? As I have outlined before, the Stockdale Paradox neatly explains why adopting an unrealistically optimistic expectation of one's situation poses major risks. Yet, it seems, human nature predisposes many people to this type of thinking. Every now and then, however, misplaced optimism gets rewarded. I am reminded of the classic film, The Cincinnati Kid. Once again, my thanks go to Wikipedia for the description.

> *The Cincinnati Kid* is a 1965 American drama film. It tells the story of Eric "The Kid" Stoner, a young Depression-era poker player, as he seeks to establish his reputation as the best. This quest leads him to challenge Lancey "The Man" Howard, an older player widely considered to be the best, culminating in a climactic final poker hand between the two.

The unlikely nature of the final hand is discussed by Anthony Holden in his book <u>*Big Deal: A Year as a Professional Poker Player*</u>, "the odds against any full house losing to any straight flush, in a two-handed game, are 45,102,781 to 1," with Holden continuing that the odds against the particular final hand in the movie are astronomical (as both hands include 10s). Holden states that the chances of both such hands appearing in one deal are "a laughable" 332,220,508,619 to 1 (more than 332 billion to 1 against) and goes on: "If these two played 50 hands of stud an hour, eight hours a day, five days a week, the situation would arise about once every 443 years." "The Man" bet his hand at each turn of the cards as if he knew he was going to hit the jackpot. Yet, each time he bet he was making an enormous miscalculation. A good poker player would have folded his hand. But "The Man" didn't and eventually won. His unrealistic expectation of hitting his hand led him to the biggest win ever. Against astronomical odds, he bet his hand heavily.

Now, it may be going too far to say that the odds of a benign outcome to the current economic outlook are as unlikely as Lancey "The Man" Howard's chances of drawing a straight flush, but every now and then it happens! And for that reason, it is worth exploring what type of factors would come into play for it to happen and what that would mean for SWAG assets.

For such a benign outcome to occur, economies across the OECD (without any priming from quantitative easing) need to see a dramatic improvement in productivity. Companies need to start investing in new projects and hiring. Governments need to start incentivising the private sector rather than creating red tape. According to Martin Sorrell, the founder of WPP - the largest advertising agency in the world:

> Western-based multi-nationals are said to have over $2 trillion in cash on their balance sheets, but unemployment remains at stubbornly high levels, with only increases in temporary employment and limited expansion of fixed capacity in Western markets. Hence, a willingness to invest in the brand and maintaining or increasing market share, rather than increasing capacity and fixed expenses.

Given that households and governments in the OECD have such a large overhanging debt burden, it is unlikely that the engine of future economic growth will derive from that source. Rather, with such large amounts of cash sitting on balance sheets, it is perhaps the corporate sector that will lead the charge for growth. The cash on balance sheets represents future potential investment and with it future potential hiring. Once hiring starts to take place, one can envisage the sort of virtuous cycle of developments that has typified economic recovery in the past. Only once unemployment stops rising might the animal spirits of recovery take a firmer grip.

Alternatively, another engine of growth that is widely touted is from the emerging economies. The debt problems centre on the OECD bloc. Emerging economies are seemingly free to expand. As the critical mass of the emerging economies rises, their respective ability to drive global growth will grow. At the current juncture, the OECD bloc probably still represents too big an end-market for emerging economy products for the emerging economies to drive growth sufficiently. Indeed, it is perhaps more likely that OECD weakness drags the emerging bloc weaker. Nonetheless, one cannot rule out the possibility that endogenous emerging market growth provides enough stimulus to the OECD to help pull the latter out of its growth slump.

If any of these positive developments took place, then plausibly, economic growth could revive enough to stabilise the deteriorating debt situation faced by OECD governments. Corporate tax revenues would rise. Unemployment payments would fall. Income tax receipts would rise. This would be the perfect outcome. I would put the probability of such an outcome at less than 10%, but that would still be considerably higher than Lancey "The Man" would have needed. It is worth clarifying that I place a low probability on a Goldilocks outcome occurring <u>in the absence of highly stimulatory quantitative easing policies being adopted</u>.

How would SWAG assets perform in such an environment? Well, in such a perfect outcome, equity assets would do tremendously well. The asset class that would potentially suffer most within SWAGs would be gold as a big part of its value is its insurance component against economic disaster. However, one could expect reasonable performances from the other SWAG assets. Silver may prove a real joker in the pack in such a scenario as a strong industrial revival may well play to silver's growing industrial use. Indeed, silver prices could go materially higher. In a world of growing prosperity one would also expect the "Billionaire effect" to assert itself and assets like art and wine would also potentially fare reasonably well as wealth effects unfolded.

In relative terms, I think equities would fare best in a very positive macro environment. In absolute terms, gold may well fall. In relative terms silver, art and wine would all probably be fine. SWAGs would not register the type of performance that has been typical over recent years, but their inclusion in a portfolio should not be damaging to the overall portfolio, adding diversification and potentially some positive though probably unspectacular results.

Why do I believe that such a Goldilocks scenario is only a sub-10% probability? To assess the risk of the scenario, it is important to understand why it is seen as so unlikely. Scarcely a week goes by without some new negative twist unfolding amongst one of the PIGS (Portugal, Italy, Greece, and Spain). If it is not a government collapsing or a new high in bond yields, it is news of mass demonstrations or some other reflection of the debacle that has beset the EMU project. Credit rating agencies need to sprint with their downgrades in order to keep up with the respective deteriorations in the economies. European policy-makers appear to be in a state of bewilderment. I am reminded of the classic final scene in the film "The Candidate" where, on achieving his objectives, a bewildered Robert Redford turns around to his adviser and asks, "What do we do now?" Policy-makers seem to be in that same state of bewilderment, not knowing quite what to do next. Bail-out funds? Debt-restructuring? Fiscal reform? Blame?

European politicians can impose a single currency. They can impose a single interest rate. They can even try to impose a uniform fiscal policy. However, in the grand scheme of things, they have missed one absolutely crucial ingredient – a harmonisation of work ethic. The politicians will never be able to impose a harmonised work ethic across economies. Some countries are just more productive than others. I will use only figures released by the OECD. In the unlikely event that someone thinks I am accusing the PIGS of being lazy, they will need to take it up with the OECD. Good luck getting through any time after 3pm, by the way.

Over the period 2000-2010, Portugal, Italy and Spain lost competitiveness against Germany. The following graph plots the relative change in unit labour costs compared with Germany. As the graph shows, Spain and Italy have

lost over 30% competitiveness relative to Germany with
Portugal some 10% worse. Data for Greece suggests a loss
of around 20%. This scale of competitiveness loss imposes
a heavy burden on each economy.

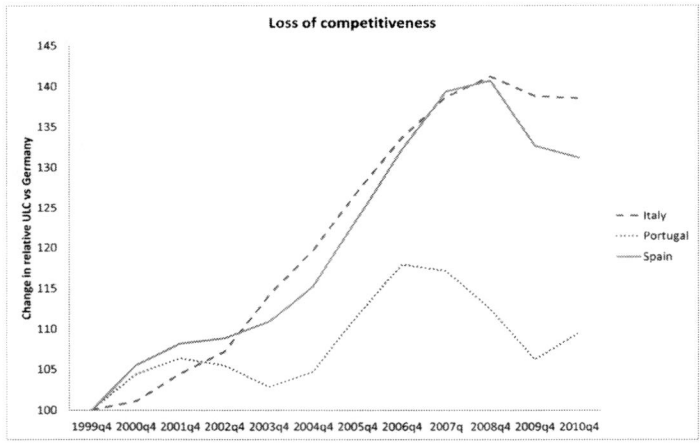

According to the OECD, the average German produces
significantly more output each year than the average
worker in the PIGS-bloc.

GDP per worker, USD current prices, 2009	
Germany	36,340
Portugal	24,980
Italy	32,408
Greece	29,368
Spain	32,254

However, this difference could simply be because the working hours for the Germans are longer. The following table, however, suggests that the problem is somewhat different.

GDP per hour worked, USD current prices, 2009	
Germany	53.1
Portugal	30.8
Italy	44.3
Greece	34.2
Spain	46.7

According to the OECD, then, German workers produce more for every hour that they work relative to the PIGS-bloc. Germany, of course, does not top the table in terms of productivity. Holland, Austria and Luxembourg all come in higher. It could be argued that such a difference in productivity reflects life-style choices. It may well reflect that, but if a unilateral policy setting is imposed on each country, inevitable frictions will arise. The objective of monetary and political union is not supposed to be a transfer of wealth from high productivity economies to low productivity economies.

Back in the original early-1990s ERM crisis, this type of divergence in competitiveness put such a strain on the ERM that widespread devaluations were forced in order to restore competitiveness. Now, of course, that option is not available. Harmonising exchange rates, interest rates and fiscal policy are necessary conditions for economic union to work. They are not sufficient. A harmonisation of work ethic is also necessary. For EMU to work, a harmonisation of productivity between EMU nations needs to be sought through policies that encourage that.

Sooner or later, the German worker is going to wonder why he is working so hard when the (rising) taxes he generates end up bailing out the economic mess within the (less *productive*) PIGS-bloc. Sooner or later, the German worker is going to realise that hard policy choices for the PIGS will always be an issue for mañana. How long before the German worker starts wondering if he, too, deserves a siesta? Bail-outs provide a massive disincentive against German productivity gains.

Plausibly, under the current policy plans, productivity will harmonise. This could happen. Pigs might fly. If it did happen, the most likely scenario is with German productivity being forced down through more and more taxation, red tape and government interference. The exact opposite needs to happen. The PIGS-bloc needs to see a very different policy prescription. Higher productivity needs to be encouraged. Governments need to become less involved. Public spending needs to be cut. Taxes need to be cut. Corporates need to be encouraged to invest. Productivity harmonisation needs to see the PIGS raise their productivity to German levels rather than see German levels lowered to that of the PIGS. The concluding part of George Orwell's Animal Farm springs to mind:

> The pigs and farmers return to their amiable card game, and the other animals creep away from the window. Soon the sounds of a quarrel draw them back to listen. Napoleon and Pilkington have played the ace of spades simultaneously, and each accuses the other of cheating. The animals, watching through the window, realize with a start that, as they look around the room of the farmhouse, they can no longer distinguish which of the card players are pigs and which are human beings.

What if the economic outlook is worse than expected?

The Goldilocks outcome of a sustainable and reasonable economic recovery has less than a 10% probability in my opinion. The alternative scenario that should be examined is the one where the debt default scenario is not cured by a debasement of the currency or via inflation but rather by outright default. An example is perhaps useful.

Imagine an individual buys a house for £500,000 on a mortgage of 90% and invests all the remainder of his assets to pay the last 10% for the house. The house is worth £500,000 and there is a mortgage of £450,000 on that house. The individual has £50,000 of his savings invested in the house. Mortgage rates are 10%, implying an annual mortgage cost of £45,000.

Now imagine that the house falls in value by 40%, making it worth £300,000. Technically, the man is now insolvent. If the mortgage company forced the man to sell the house, he would be unable to pay off all the debt, making him insolvent. However, so long as the man keeps his job and continues paying the annual mortgage cost of £45,000, then technically although he is insolvent, he is not illiquid.

The difference between insolvent and illiquid is an important distinction. Most of today's policy prescriptions misdiagnose the problem. Europe's sovereign debt crisis is constantly treated as a problem of just liquidity rather than solvency and liquidity. The result is that the misdiagnosis results in the application of the wrong medicine. Each time a new bail-out is granted that allows a problem-economy to pay off the coupons on its (mortgage) debt, analysts and politicians claim a line-in-the-sand has been drawn and the crisis averted. This, of course, is completely false. Europe's problem is a combination of illiquidity AND insolvency. Bail-outs only delay the D-Day. Default-Day.

Faced with a situation where a government spends more than it earns, it needs to borrow. By borrowing, it issues bonds that it expects investors to buy, thereby lending the government the money to bridge the gap between their excess spending and their revenues. But what happens to a government when nobody wants to buy the bonds they issue? Well, one result could be that interest rates need to rise in order to entice investors to buy the bonds. However, if for whatever reasons investors just do not want to buy the bonds, governments have the power to simply print more money and lend that money back to themselves. Governments never need to declare illiquidity or insolvency. There is always the printing press that can be used so that a government avoids default. Governments always have that option. Well, that isn't strictly true.

Thanks to the European Monetary Union, an unknown factor has been introduced into the fray regarding sovereign default. If, for example, Portugal faced a situation where it couldn't issue its bonds, Portugal does not have the capacity to print Euros and lend those Euros back to itself in order to buy the bonds it has just issued. The European Union prevents such action as it is not in the interests of the EMU economies to allow unrestricted national printing of Euros. Only the European Central Bank (ECB) can print Euros. This throws an enormous spanner into the works for a country facing illiquidity and insolvency issues. In fact, it throws two enormous spanners. First, it prevents the printing of money to overcome the default risk and second it also technically prevents the unrestricted depreciation of the currency that would achieve the same ends. A substantially weaker exchange rate has the effect of boosting competitiveness thereby injecting growth into an economy. This could make an enormous difference to how the European crisis unfolds.

At this juncture, it is worth exploring some of the research conducted by the IMF. Back in July 2000 following the Asian crises, the IMF produced a report entitled "Currency and Banking Crises: The Early Warnings of Distress". The study looked at 102 financial episodes in 20 countries.

The IMF went back to the drawing board again in the November 2008 treatise "Systemic Banking Crises: A new database". In this paper, the IMF examined all systemically important banking collapses for the period 1970-2007. There were 42 in total covering 37 countries. According to the IMF, although there will always be exceptions, financial crises do tend to display specific characteristics.

The IMF's findings provide some interesting data on crisis economies ahead of that crisis starting. Prior to a financial crisis starting, the average fiscal balance is a deficit of 2.1% of GDP and the current account typically tends to be in deficit to tune of 3.9% of GDP.

Some 70% of economies that ran into crisis were already running budget deficits, while some 86% were already running current account deficits. A prior loss of export competitiveness would also be another factor that would be worth highlighting as part of a typical crisis DNA.

The on-going problems in Europe carry the same DNA as so many of the IMF's sample crisis cases. Compare the IMF statistics with Spain's current economic position. Spain currently runs a budget deficit of over 6% of GDP and a current account deficit of 5% of GDP. Its debt-to-GDP ratio has risen from 42% of GDP in 2007 to a predicted 78% in 2011. Over the last decade, Spain's export competitiveness has deteriorated by some 25%.

According to the OECD, Spain has the highest structural unemployment in the OECD bloc by a wide margin.

It also has one of the lowest estimated potential GDP growth rates. Only Iceland and Greece are lower.

In the 1990s, Finland faced an almost identical set of statistics amidst a banking crisis. Finland's initial steps onto the hard core path were based on a significant boost to competitiveness via a currency depreciation combined with draconian (and enduring) fiscal retrenchment. Imposing austere fiscal restraint without offering an accompanying boost to competitiveness via a weaker exchange rate runs the risk of creating a debt deflation scenario as restrictive fiscal policy may just end up weakening growth further resulting in more cyclically generated budget deficits.

An unsustainable debt dynamic may be the result. As George Soros put it,

"The European Union will suffer something worse than a lost decade as it will endure a chronic divergence in which the surplus countries forge ahead and the deficit countries are dragged down by their accumulated debt burden."

The success of many of the IMF's historical policy "prescriptions" for countries in crisis is reflected in the duality between fiscal austerity and competitiveness boost. They went hand-in-hand. Europe's single currency precludes such an option. Given the scale of fiscal austerity being imposed on the domestic economy, Spain faces a race between its ability to export its way out of trouble and the deleterious cyclical effect on its budget deficit from a weak domestic economy.

Had there been a 20% competitiveness gain (as indeed Finland enjoyed in the early 1990s), one might argue that Spain had a chance of engineering a strong export performance. In the absence of such a competitiveness gain, and with OECD economies generally in the midst of significant fiscal restraint themselves, Spanish fault lines look set to be exposed.

The UK or US would always have an option to print more of their domestic currency so that a default in local currency terms is avoided. The Eurozone doesn't necessarily have that option. If Spain or Italy or Portugal can't pay their debts it is by no means certain that the ECB will sanction a mass-printing of Euros to debase the problem away. Further, without that excess printing of Euros, a competitiveness boost via a weakening Euro seems unlikely.

This puts Spain and EMU countries like it in a very difficult corner. Faced with insolvency and illiquidity, they cannot print their way out of trouble nor can they engineer a competitiveness gain through a weakening Euro. The Goldilocks scenario is to see such economies grow their way out of trouble via sheer hard work and productivity gains. The alternative is a debt default. Thanks to the very nature of EMU, such a scenario is very possible. I put the probability of such a scenario at comfortably over 10%. Maybe even up to 20%.

Such a scenario would be catastrophic for the global economy as it would almost certainly make the US sub-prime crisis look like an amuse-bouche. In a financial meltdown, most assets would become worth fractions of their former values. Obviously, government bonds in defaulted zones become worthless. The risk of multi-bank failures would see credit spreads widen dramatically and all but the most secure bonds would suffer. Equities? Forget them. Or at the very minimum, wait until they have dropped at least 50% before letting that Stockdale Paradox get the better of you.

SWAGs? In such an environment, all assets will likely be crushed. Gold and silver, however, will most likely hold up well against most asset classes. In a true meltdown, gold could become extremely important as one can only assume a re-working of capitalism would need to include a more formal role for gold going forward. One can see a situation where once the dust had settled, economists and politicians would realise that the true bubble was in the supply of paper money and that a stronger foundation would be needed to allow capitalism to work in the future. Gold (and probably silver) would hold up well in such a scenario. Art and wine? In reality, both assets would likely suffer, but since both assets are tangible and carry SWAG properties, they do not have an associated risk of defaulting to a zero worth. Countries where currencies have remained strong may see fantastic opportunities to acquire iconic art and wines. There will always be winners in a financial meltdown. No doubt such winners will be accumulating SWAGs.

Hyper-inflation scenario

Hyper-inflation is not as rare as many believe. The 1920s Weimar Republic of Germany is often quoted as the classic example of a hyper-inflation. Yet, over the last twenty years there have been plenty of other examples ranging from Angola, Belarus, Brazil, Mexico, Poland, Russia, and most recently Zimbabwe. Hyper-inflation is spectacular in its effect, but it is not especially rare. Perhaps one of the better books written on hyper-inflation is called "Monetary Regimes and Inflation: History, Economic and Political Relationships" by Peter Bernholz. Bernholz identifies some 29 different periods of hyper-inflation and writes in detail about 12 of them.

There is no question that hyper-inflation would solve the problem of a sovereign debt default. Think of it like this; a man with a house worth £400,000 and a mortgage of £300,000 has a salary of £40,000 per annum and a mortgage cost of £4000 per annum. Now assume in a hyper-inflation that everything trebles with the exception of the size of the mortgage debt. Now the house is worth £1.2m. The man's salary is £120,000 per annum. His mortgage debt of £300,000 now looks much more manageable. This is the wonder of inflation! It works for those with high leverage. And in most cases, it is the choice method of governments for dealing with excess government debt. As John Mauldin writes in one of his weekly reports:

> You don't even have to go that far back to see hyperinflation and how brilliantly it works at eliminating debt. Let's look at the example of Brazil, which is one of the world's most recent examples of hyperinflation. Today Brazil has very little debt as it has all been inflated away. Its economy is booming, people trust the central bank and the country is a

success story. Much like the United States had high inflation in the 1970s and then got a diligent central banker like Paul Volcker, in Brazil a new government came in, beat inflation, produced strong real GDP growth and set the stage for one of the greatest economic success stories of the past two decades. Indeed the same could be said of other countries like Turkey that had hyperinflation, devaluation, and then found monetary and fiscal rectitude.

In 1993 Brazilian inflation was roughly 2,000%. Only four years later, in 1997 it was 7%. Almost as if by magic, the debt disappeared. Imagine if the US increased its money supply which is currently $900 billion by a factor of 10,000 times as Brazil's did between 1991 and 1996. We would have 9 quadrillion USD on the Fed's balance sheet. That is a lot of zeros. It would also mean that our current debt of thirteen trillion would be chump change. A critic of this strategy for getting rid of our debt could point out that no one would lend to us again if we did that. Hardly. Investors, sadly, have very short memories. Markets always forgive default and inflation. Just look at Brazil, Bolivia, and Russia today. Foreigners are delighted to invest in these countries.

To get some handle on how rapidly hyperinflation works Steve Hanke, Professor of Applied Economics at The John Hopkins University and Senior Fellow at The Cato Institute produced the "New Hyperinflation Index". The following table details Hanke's index of the worst cases of hyperinflation:

Highest Monthly Inflation Rates in History				
Country	Month with highest inflation rate	Highest monthly inflation rate	Equivalent daily inflation rate	Time required for prices to double
Hungary	July 1946	1.30×10^{16}%	195%	15.6 hours
Zimbabwe	Mid-November 2008 (latest measurable)	79,600,000,000%	98.0%	24.7 hours
Yugoslavia	January 1994	313,000,000%	64.6%	1.4 days
Germany	October 1923	29,500%	20.9%	3.7 days
Greece	November 1944	11,300%	17.1%	4.5 days
China	May 1949	4,210%	13.4%	5.6 days

The current OECD bloc sees inflation measured as a change compared with a year ago (and increases of more than 3% seen as on the high side). In the worst cases of hyperinflation, price changes need to be viewed on a daily basis, with instances of prices doubling inside a day.

In Weimar Germany in the 1920s episode of hyperinflation, a loaf of bread cost 163 Marks in 1922. By September 1923, this figure had reached 1,500,000 Marks and at the peak of hyperinflation, November 1923, a loaf of bread cost 200,000,000,000 Marks.

In 1920, the highest valued stamp issued by the German postal office was 4 Marks. By 1923, the denominations were changing so frequently that the post office could not design new stamps fast enough and resorted to using old dies and over-printing them with new values. The highest price reached in 1923 was for 50,000,000,000 Marks.

One amusing anecdote tells the story of a student at Frieburg University who ordered a cup of coffee at a café. The price on the menu was 5,000 Marks. He had two cups. When the bill came, it was for 14,000 Marks. On questioning the bill, the student was told, "If you want to save money, and you want two cups of coffee, you should order them both at the same time."

And, if there is any doubt how such inflations hurt the poorer members of society, there are plenty of anecdotes showing this clearly. Ernest Hemingway recounts a story from his time in Germany in 1922:

> Our first purchase was from a fruit stand beside the main street of Kehl where an old woman was selling apples, peaches and plums. We picked out five very good looking apples and gave the old woman a 50 Mark note. She gave us back 38 Marks in exchange. A very nice looking, white bearded old gentlemen saw us buy the apples and raised his hat. "Pardon me, sir," he said, rather timidly in German, "how much were the apples?"
>
> I counted the change and told him 12 Marks.
>
> He smiled and shook his head. "I can't pay it. It is too much."

He went up the street....I wish I had offered him some. Twelve Marks, on that day, amounted to a little under two cents. The old man, whose life's savings were probably, as most of the non-profiteer classes are, invested in German pre-war and war bonds, could not afford a 12-Mark expenditure.

As interesting as these historical anecdotes are, and as many analysts have argued, isn't this hyperinflation risk more of a historical relic that will not be allowed to happen in a modern economy, especially given all the central bank knowledge that is available today?

It is certainly true that smart analysts have argued that since the velocity with which money passes around the economy has fallen so much (presumably reflecting a lack of animal spirits), as well as the fact that in order for hyperinflation to occur governments would need to be inordinately incompetent, the odds of a bout of hyperinflation comparable with the worst cases in history do seem remote.

First, I would not bet against a government being inordinately incompetent, especially when such incompetence has a self-interest attached to it. Second, a hyperinflation event does not have to be of the jaw-dropping nature of 1940s Hungary or 1920s Germany. A modern hyperinflation could be an altogether more moderate affair. One cannot rule it out simply because replicating history seems unlikely. Secondly, in most hyperinflations, velocity is driven higher out of necessity.

The very moment that wages are paid drives employees to find goods to buy before prices have risen again. To argue that low velocity will prevent hyperinflation looks at the problem from the wrong angle. Hyperinflation will necessitate higher velocity – people will need to spend their cash quickly to prevent inflation eroding its buying power.

The central case of this book assumes that the extraordinary bouts of money printing now taking place will lead to bouts of inflation within economies indulging most in that money printing process. That central scenario would see quite a decent rise in inflation, but does not envisage the type of hyperinflation seen in Weimar Germany. It would envisage, perhaps, prices doubling over a decade. But a hyperinflation is of a different order altogether, seeing prices double over a year (if not a day!). Could such a situation evolve within the OECD bloc?

Evidence to support this scenario can be found in Peter Bernholz's book. According to Bernholz:

> Hyperinflations are <u>always</u> caused by public budget deficits which are largely financed by money creation.

Well, that certainly rings a warning bell.

Bernholz went on to suggest that there has appeared to be a critical level of debt beyond which hyperinflations become more likely. According to his study of 12 specific examples of hyperinflation that had detailed data, Bernholz concluded that:

> In all cases of hyperinflation, deficits amounting to more than 20% of public expenditures are present, is confirmed for all cases except Belarus, Turkmenistan, Poland and Yugoslavia. Whereas the first three shows deficits of between 5.87% and 12.04% of expenditures

To put this finding into context, the following table looks at some prevailing budget deficits expressed as a percentage of government expenditure, as per the Bernholz concept and looks at the most recent completed year relative to the last 15 years or so of history.

Government deficits as % of public spending	1994-2001 average	2002-2009 average	2010
US	2.8%	13.1%	24.9%
UK	4.2%	9.4%	18.8%
Greece	12.4%	14.8%	17.2%
Spain	8.4%	3.5%	20.4%
Japan	16.7%	14.0%	19.0%

Money creation is being used to finance government deficits. Further, some major economies are flirting with deficit to spending ratios of around 20%. It is not unreasonable to see why a potential hyperinflation scenario is at least on the radar.

What probability, then, of a hyperinflation within the OECD economies? If an outright debt-default scenario carries a probability of 10-20%, and a Goldilocks "everything will be just great" scenario carries a probability of 10%, one would have to put the probability of a hyperinflation scenario within one of the major OECD economies at 5-10%. It is an outside bet, but one that needs to be factored into the risk profile.

In such a world, owning physical assets like SWAGs will prove a highly effective way of protecting value. Assets like bonds will be wiped out. The indiscriminate nature of hyperinflation will also wipe out many good businesses rendering equity ownership a volatile proposition. Hard physical assets will outperform in this type of world. Of course, in such a world it is impossible to predict anything with any degree of comfort. Physical assets, however, should provide some insulation against the worst of hyperinflation. What is most likely to happen, however, is that necessity goods become of greater importance. The availability of the supply of food and basic essentials becomes somewhat more pressing than having a cellar full of wine. Will the physical assets in SWAG act as a good form of money in such a world? One can only believe that silver and gold will act like hard money.

Marc Faber's prophetic book "Tomorrow's Gold" highlights an interesting observation about the performance of equities during a hyperinflation. During the onset of hyperinflation, equity investments may best be avoided. However, there comes a point where equity investments become extremely cheap amidst the eye of the hyperinflation storm. Faber calls this the "inflation paradox". Faber argues that it is quite typical during hyperinflations for equities to become extremely undervalued. Faber gives many examples and his book is very much worth reading. The following is taken from Faber's description of the 1977-87 Argentinian and 1991-94 Peruvian hyperinflations:

> **Argentina**
>
> Molinos, which could have been bought in 1987 for as little as $20m, was worth $515m in 1994; and Picardo, which sold for a mere $12m in 1986, had reached $213m.
>
> **Peru**
>
> Between 1991 and 1994, under President Alberto Fujimori, Peru experienced a similar turnaround. Inflation fell from over 1000% per annum to less than 10%, its market capitalisation rose from around $600m to $5bn.

Hyperinflation brings with it enormous uncertainty. As Bernholz concludes:

> High inflations do not promote growth of GDP and lower unemployment except perhaps in the beginning. At the height of hyperinflation, growth is negative and unemployment increases.

It is certainly the case that fixed income bonds and equity assets are likely to fare badly during the onset of a hyperinflation. It brings with it heightened social unrest and high degrees of financial volatility. In a world that has become very burdened with debt, such volatility will be very problematic. Physical assets such as gold and silver will likely maintain purchasing power as well as any asset in such a situation. In the teeth of that crisis, however, as Faber suggests, the optimum strategy is to look to buy highly distressed and extremely undervalued equities, presumably with the gold and silver that have appreciated enormously as the crisis has unfolded. The ability to time these events, however, is likely to be extremely difficult.

Summary Chapter 17

- Economics is about gauging probabilities. The outlook is always a range of different possibilities. Nothing is impossible. Whenever one makes a long-term bet on an asset class, it is important to remain flexible in case the economic environment envisaged turns out to be different to the one expected.

- A range of alternative economic scenarios can unfold over the coming decade. How would some alternative outcomes affect SWAG assets?

- In a Goldilocks scenario, in the absence of the need for quantitative easing, where everything turns out well, growth revives, budget deficits return to balance and productivity improves, then equities clearly would be a major beneficiary. Gold's role as "house insurance" would no doubt suffer in such a world. Silver would likely benefit from its growing role as an industrial metal. One could only assume that such a benign environment would see global wealth increases provide firm support for wine and art. Overall, one would expect SWAGs to perform well in an absolute sense but almost certainly less well than equities in a relative sense. Probability of a Goldilocks scenario? 10%.

- An alternative scenario is one where the economic environment is much worse with a sovereign default-led crisis creating a debt-deflation scenario. Banking systems would collapse. Such an environment would see a collapse in most assets in absolute terms. In relative terms, any asset that can maintain its tangibility will be useful in such an environment. Gold and silver, in particular, may prove very positive assets relative to lower credit bonds and equities. Probability of this type of world? 10-20%.

- The third alternative is one of hyperinflation. Hyperinflation just isn't as rare as most people believe. The factors that can create a hyperinflation are certainly in evidence across many major economies. In a hyperinflation the ownership of fixed income assets is a disaster. Equity ownership is also fraught with risk. Physical assets are king in such an environment. SWAGs would insulate wealth should such a situation develop. Probability of a hyperinflation in one of the major OECD economies is 5-10%.

CHAPTER 18

How to Do it

Constructing a portfolio brings three big problems. First,
what assets should be included? Second, what weights to
attach to specific assets? And third, how regularly to
change those weights? The subject of creating a portfolio
is complex enough to write a book about in itself. In fact,
so many have been written and with such diverse views,
it would be pointless to even touch upon the subject here.
To summarise a very complex subject, one can say that
there are two main schools of thought.

The first school of thought is what I call the Tim Leslie
approach. Tim Leslie is one of the smartest portfolio
managers I have met. He now runs his own fund
but several years ago spent time at Moore Capital.
I remember a meeting with him once with the head of
risk management. The latter was giving a lecture on the
importance of diversification. Tim listened intently. At
the end of the lecture, Tim sat for a few seconds and then
said the following. "I have many books on portfolio
construction. Whenever I get a new book on the subject,
the very first thing I do is go straight to the chapter on
diversification". The Head of Risk Management was

clearly impressed. But then Tim added, "…..and then the next thing I do is rip that entire chapter out of the book and throw it in the rubbish bin."

One can keep all of one's eggs in one basket. Or, one can have many baskets. But if all the eggs are in just one basket, one needs to watch that basket very closely. Tim is that type of portfolio manager. He believes in concentrating his investments in a few highly selected ideas. He does not believe it is possible to outperform the market by having a widely-diversified portfolio.

Other portfolio managers will adopt an altogether different approach where a portfolio is diversified across many different types of asset class and even within a specific asset class there is a great deal of diversification.

Each approach has its advantages and disadvantages. Of course there is an infinite number of shades of grey in-between. My approach to portfolio management errs more towards the latter though I would say that when a particular idea seems very strong I will tend to nuance that idea with a higher weight in the portfolio. An over-riding principle governs my approach, however, and that is capital preservation.

As I mentioned before, I do not believe that any asset in itself is too risky. Rather, the risk to capital preservation comes when too much weight is given to a specific asset. Assets that tend to have enormous volatility should, generally speaking, not hold a huge weight in a portfolio as the risk of capital loss will be significant. If an investor is happy having that exposure because he also wants the risk of making high returns, then that is an elected preference for a specific risk.

There is no right or wrong, then, in portfolio creation. Some investors will want their portfolios to display certain characteristics while others will want other types of characteristics. With that caveat in mind, my own preference is to see SWAG assets occupy a 20+% weighting in an overall portfolio. This weighting is based on the economic expectations that have been highlighted in this book. In ten years' time, such a weighting may be inappropriate. I would say that while a fiat money system is in place, there should always be some place in a portfolio for SWAG assets.

Within the specific SWAG assets, I would tend to weight the assets quite equally. This is just my personal choice and others will, I am sure, have a variation or personal preference that suits them better.

With these guidelines in place, the question then arises of how, exactly, would an investor implement a SWAG strategy into their portfolio. There are two approaches. For a very large fund, the best method is via direct investment. By this, I mean owning the specific assets in a physical form. Gold and silver can be purchased in physical form and stored relatively cheaply in vaults specifically designed for purpose. Wine is likewise easy to purchase and store in bonded warehouses that keep the wine in perfect condition at a relatively low cost. Art can also be purchased directly and stored in correct conditions. There are a number of advisory companies that act to both recommend and provide storage for art and wine.

For the average investor, however, such a process makes
no sense. According to the Credit Suisse Global Wealth
Report, the average (median) wealth in the UK is around
$122,000 per head. In the US, it is just $52,000 per head.
With a portfolio that is small, buying art becomes a
problem because unlike wine, silver and gold, art tends
to be "lumpy" and a single piece of art can amount to a
disproportionate part of a small portfolio. Instead, an
investor with a smaller portfolio needs to find ways of
gaining access to art on a smaller scale. That does not
mean buying lower value pieces of art. That would
almost certainly be a mistake from an investment
perspective. Rather, the objective should be to gain
access to the most investable art, but through some form
of managed fund. Silver and gold pose less of a problem
since access to movements in gold and silver can be
achieved through the many Exchange Traded Funds
(ETFs) that deal directly in gold and silver. Such ETFs
also cover a vast array of other metals including
platinum. For the private investor, ETFs represent a good
way of getting access to the precious metals. Likewise,
there are many vehicles which offer investment in high
grade wine.

More and more art and wine funds are emerging that
give access to smaller portfolios. If one Googles "Wine
Fund", a whole host of possible investment vehicles are
offered. Liv-Ex provides unparalleled information about
the wine market and is unbiased in its presentation of
information. On its website, it describes itself as the
global marketplace for fine wine with members in 33
countries. For a potential investor, Liv-Ex would
certainly be one plausible and reputable starting point.

The Liv-Ex index of 100 investment grade wines has been included on Bloomberg Indices and is the industry benchmark for fine wine prices. Liv-Ex provides information on many angles of wine investment.

According to Fine Art Wealth Management, a year or so ago there were only 12 art funds active globally. Today there are some 40 different art investment vehicles in different stages of development. The longest running fund, "The Fine Art Fund", established in 2001, has produced an annual internal rate of return of 25% on sold assets between 2004 and 2011. The first of its six funds, a 10-year fund specialising in western art, also called The Fine Art Fund, started distributing proceeds to investors in 2009. The Collectors Fund, a US-based fund founded three years ago, also offers a 10-year private equity-type fund that buys American masters. The fund has already sold some works, and Sandy Kemper, its founder and chairman, says the fund has a 28.5% realised net IRR. Meanwhile, the Collection of Modern Art, an open investment fund set up by alternative asset manager Castlestone Management in 2009, has a collection of 32 art works by post-war blue-chip artists and has generated a 7.5% annualised return. Again, investors who are interested in allocating a portion of their assets to art will need to do their own due diligence on the investment managers they choose to use.

Different managers will offer different things. It is certainly the case, though, that there is now an avenue for investment in art for the small investor. Fine Art Wealth Management are a company that aims to evaluate the art market as well as provide an investment platform for potential investors to gain access to art. That may be a good starting point for research. I think it is important to say that I am not recommending any specific fund. I have no investments in any of the funds mentioned and therefore strongly recommend any investor to do their own research into whether a specific fund fits their specific requirements. The fact is, there are a number of vehicles now available that allow both institutional as well as small investor the opportunity to gain exposure to SWAG assets.

Summary Chapter 18

- Portfolio construction is a complex subject. One can keep all of one's eggs in one basket. Or, one can have many baskets. Each approach has its advantages and disadvantages, with an infinite number of shades of grey in-between. My approach to portfolio management errs more towards the latter, with an over-riding principle of capital preservation.

- There is no right or wrong, then, in portfolio construction – just personal preference. With that caveat in mind, my own preference is to see SWAG assets occupy a 20-30% weighting in an overall portfolio. This weighting is based on the economic expectations that have been highlighted in this book. In ten years' time, such a weighting may be inappropriate. I would say that while a fiat money system is in place, there should always be some place in a portfolio for SWAG assets.

- Within the specific SWAG assets, I would tend to weight the assets equally. This is just my personal choice and others will, I am sure, have a variation or personal preference that suits them better.

- The question then arises of how, exactly, would an investor implement a SWAG strategy into their portfolio. There are two approaches. For a very large fund, the best method is via direct investment. By this, I mean owning the specific assets in a physical form. Specialist advisers can be found in this respect.

- For the average investor, however, such a process makes no sense. With a portfolio that is small, buying art becomes a problem because unlike wine, silver and gold, art tends to be "lumpy" and a single piece of art can amount to a disproportionate part of a small portfolio. Instead, an investor with a smaller portfolio needs to find ways of gaining access to art on a smaller scale.

- According to Fine Art Wealth Management, a year or so ago there were only 12 art funds active globally. Today there are some 40 different art investment vehicles in different stages of development. Investors who are interested in allocating a portion of their assets to art will need to do their own due diligence on the investment managers they choose to use. Different managers will offer different things. It is certainly the case, though, that there is now an avenue for investment in art for the small investor.

- Private investors also have the option to allocate to some SWAGs and not others. Investors should feel free to select which characteristics are most suitable to their specific portfolio and desired return profile and horizon.

CHAPTER 19

It is All About Robustness

Through an indispensable requirement for the functioning of an extensive order of cooperation of free people, money has almost from its first appearance been so shamelessly abused by governments that it has become the prime source of disturbance of all self-ordering processes in the extended order of human cooperation. The history of government management of money has, except for a few short happy periods, been one of incessant fraud and deception. In this respect, governments have proved far more immoral than any private agency supplying distinct kinds of money in competition could have been. F.A. Hayek - The Fatal Conceit

Like Rothbard, Hayek had a healthy disdain for government. Those that sympathise with government may just dismiss the likes of Hayek and Rothbard as ivory tower economists with no sense of everyday practicality. An inspection of the facts would suggest that closer scrutiny of government policy is needed.

The bottom line is that most governments in the OECD have been guilty of the grossest incompetence.

Sometimes, the occasional act of incompetence is understandable. After all, economics is an imprecise science and governments are, after all, only human. However, when an incompetence becomes ingrained, decade after decade, then it becomes unforgiveable. The current state of government finances is often blamed on the reckless bankers and the fact that massive bailouts have been needed to keep the financial sectors afloat. This is only a part of the problem. The current state of crisis is also very much the culmination of decades of public sector mismanagement. Like any prudent individual, governments should balance their books. In times of economic prosperity, governments should run budget surpluses, and in times of economic strife budget deficits. Over an entire economic cycle, governments should run close-to-balanced budgets.

Between 1980 and 2011, a total of 32 years of data, the US economy ran budget deficits on no less than 29 occasions. In the UK, there were 28 deficit years and 4 surplus years. For the OECD bloc as a whole, there were 31 deficit years and just one surplus year. The surplus year was the boom around the internet dot.com mania in 2000 when OECD GDP hit a 4.2% annual growth rate. For the last 20 years, 4.2% represents the highest rate of growth for the OECD. So, the only time in the last decade when the OECD has managed to run a budget surplus has been amidst a massive and unsustainable economic boom.

This isn't prudent government policy. It's a public sector spend-fest. In times of boom, government spend the booty. In times of bust, they borrow more. The following tables show the budget statistics and borrowing figures for the OECD bloc as a whole:

1980-2011	Number of years running budget deficits	Average size of budget deficits (% of GDP)	Number of years running budget surpluses	Average size of budget surpluses (% of GDP)
OECD	31/32	-3.4%	1/32	+0.2%
US	29/32	-4.2%	3/32	+0.8%
UK	28/32	-5.2%	4/32	+1.4%

So, not only are the deficits vastly more numerous in occurrence, but when they do happen, they are substantially bigger in size than the odd occasion when a budget surplus arrives. What is the everyday parallel to this?

To my mind, the evidence from government spending is akin to a household that consistently spends more than it earns. Every now and then, that household will enjoy a lottery win that boosts its income for that year. And, that lottery win will essentially be spent in that year and not saved. The result is that overall levels of government debt just keep rising and rising. The current crisis has been brought to a head by various specific acts of extreme recklessness, but there should be no mistake made about why economies had become so vulnerable in the first instance - gross and widespread government incompetence.

The stunning rise in household, financial and government borrowing over the 2000-2010 period created a false illusion of prosperity. Central banks became convinced of their own ability to control the business cycle. Governments allowed (almost encouraged) institutions and households to act recklessly. Yet, the reality was that OECD economies had become distinctly more vulnerable and subject to shock. As that shock emerged, the lack of economic robustness within the OECD has resulted in the crisis that currently prevails.

True to form, what has been the government response to a problem caused by too much borrowing? It beggars belief to hear economists and politicians argue that more stimulus is needed to boost demand. The problem was created in the first instance by the creation of too many things. Too many houses. Too many SUVs. Too many flatscreen TVs. The false illusion of wealth allowed households to believe that they needed and should have all these new things, even if they did not have the income to pay for them. The problem has never been about a lack of demand. The problem has been about too much supply and the artificial demand that was created by excess borrowing to satiate that excess supply. The solution to the problem is not to re-inflate the bubble by boosting demand. But, governments are incompetent. Governments would rather do the economically wrong but politically right (to gain votes). Hence the OECD economies stand at the brink of a new inflection point where governments will force a redistribution of wealth via financial repression, money printing and the generation of inflation. The savers will be called upon to bail out the over-borrowed.

One can make various intellectual and moral comments about this process. But such comments won't actually help those millions of soon-to-be pensioners and savers who will be financially whacked by the process. One of the more insightful financial books to have emerged in recent years is Nassim Taleb's "The Black Swan". Although the book usually comes under the heading of finance, it is really more philosophy. In Taleb's world, a "Black Swan" event is one that is a major surprise to the observer that has a major impact, but after the event is rationalized by hindsight as if it could have been expected.

By definition, Black Swan events cannot be predicted. Indeed, Taleb strongly recommends not trying to predict them. Instead, his suggestion is that we should recognise that Black Swan events do occur, that we will not know what they will be, but that they will impact on our lives materially. Further, he argues that the actions we should take are to build robustness against potential negative events. Following the second edition of "The Black Swan", Taleb provides a ten point checklist that attempts to create this robustness.

I have highlighted five of Taleb's ten point checklist:

1. **<u>What is fragile should break early while it's still small</u>**: Nothing should ever become too big to fail.

2. ***<u>No socialisation of losses and privatisation of gains</u>:*** Whatever may need to be bailed out should be nationalised; whatever does not need a bailout should be free, small and risk-bearing.

3. *Only Ponzi schemes should depend on confidence:*
Governments should never need to "restore
confidence". Governments cannot stop the
rumours. We just need to be able to shrug off
rumours, to be robust to them.

4. **Do not give an addict more drugs if he has
withdrawal pains:** Using leverage to cure the
problems of too much leverage is not homoeopathy,
it's denial. The debt crisis is not a temporary
problem, it's a structural one..

5. *Citizens should not depend on financial assets as
a repository of value and rely on fallible "expert"
advice for their retirement:* Economic life should
be de-financialised.

I chose these five as they almost uncannily recommend
the opposite to what is currently taking place.
Governments are now in the business of bailing-out
those who have over-borrowed (including themselves).
Governments are socialising the losses from the bail-outs
with the taxpayer at large financing the cost of the
financial bailout. Financial repression adds further to
this bailout process. Governments are indulging in
unconventional monetary policy which is akin to a Ponzi
scheme, and they see the cure for the excess borrowing
of the past to be yet even more borrowing now. Hair of
the dog. The OECD economies are in the trouble they
are in now because of decade after decade of fiscal
mismanagement. As each decade has passed, the
vulnerability to shock that the OECD economies could
withstand has diminished. If governments had wanted to
write a script that would eventually but inevitably result

in a financial crisis, they now have the means to do so as historical fact. Taleb's rules for robustness have been diametrically opposed by governments across the OECD. Yet, robustness may be one of the most valuable assets needed.

The last of Taleb's points mentioned above argues that complex financial instruments expose citizens to risks that they may just not appreciate. Taleb argues for a de-financialisation of assets where value is not warehoused inside financial markets. In this sense, I am driving at a similar goal. The fact that those in financial markets do not view SWAG assets as financial instruments must be a positive factor. SWAG assets are certainly less complex in nature and thanks to the fact that they are tangible, they offer a value which is not subject to the same black-box wizardry that so often accompanies financial assets. Taleb's point is to prepare for Black Swan events. Any financial adviser will argue that it is correct to be financially (and otherwise) robust so that whatever event occurs, some degree of preparation and anticipation proves to be valuable. Yet, in the same breath that such robustness is praised, suggested asset allocations place investors in precisely the same vulnerable asset zones that will prove anything but robust.

Against Taleb's advice, then, I am attempting to predict a Black Swan event for the advanced OECD economies. I believe that the combination of gross government fiscal incompetence, all-time high government debt/GDP ratios, an anticipated marked deterioration in the age-dependency ratio, a new dynamic restricting the supply of key raw materials and the added spice of a wide-scale usage of unconventional monetary policy provides a unique mixture of factors that create the potential for something very unusual. Each of the ingredients creates the potential for major economic disruption. However, unlike a Black Swan event, I believe what is likely to unfold may be considerably rarer. Each of the factors represents a form of economic fault line.

An "Economic Cascadia" seems a more fitting description of the current economic turmoil. Each of the ingredients that have been described in this book ranging from demographics and budget deficits to debt ratios, financial repression, quantitative easing and supply constraints represent a form of economic fault line. The pressure building up within these specific fault lines represents a slow but persistent catastrophe-in-the-making. The rupture of each fault line is almost impossible to predict. When a series of different fault lines all meet at the same point and each with pent up force, the potential for a Cascadian Moment develops. Such moments typically occur very infrequently. The advanced economies are facing a confluence of economic fault lines that have the potential to dramatically alter the economic landscape for a generation.

> The Cascadia Subduction Zone is a very long sloping fault that stretches from mid-Vancouver Island to Northern California. It separates the Juan de Fuca and North America plates. New ocean floor is being created offshore of Washington and Oregon. As more material wells up along the ocean ridge, the ocean floor is pushed toward and beneath the continent.

The Cascadia Subduction Zone is where the two plates meet.

The width of the Cascadia Subduction Zone fault varies along its length, depending on the temperature of the subducted oceanic slab, which heats up as it is pushed deeper beneath the continent. As it becomes hotter and more molten it eventually loses the ability to store mechanical stress and generate earthquakes. The "locked" zone is storing up energy for an earthquake, and the "transition" zone, although somewhat plastic, could probably rupture.

Great Subduction Zone earthquakes are the largest earthquakes in the world, and can exceed magnitude 9.0. Earthquake size is porportional to fault area, and the Cascadia Subduction Zone is a very long sloping fault that stretches from mid-Vancouver Island to Northern California. It separates the Juan de Fuca and North America plates. Because of the very large fault area, the Cascadia Subduction Zone could produce a very large earthquake, magnitude 9.0 or greater, if rupture occurred over its whole area.

The last known great earthquake in the northwest was in **January, 1700**, just over 300 years ago. Geological evidence indicates that great earthquakes may have occurred at least seven times in the last 3,500 years, suggesting a return time of 400 to 600 years.

The Pacific Northwest Seismic Network

The situation is so unique that it makes the future investment landscape extremely difficult to predict. I have come to think of the economic outlook probabilities as an inverted normal distribution, where the highest probabilities are for the most extreme events. Trend growth and subdued low inflation, which was very much par for the course in the 1980s and 1990s, now seems the most remote of probabilities. In economic jargon, the scale of disequilibrium has reached a tipping point and something has to give. Those that believe cash is a safe asset in such a world run the risk of seeing prices of goods and services around them rise rapidly. Hemingway's apple anecdote springs to mind. Those who believe government fixed income to represent a cast-iron safe investment run the same risk. Those hoping for a return to the cult of the equity may well be subject to the Stockdale Paradox. The bottom line is that there is no guarantee that any specific investment or investment style will work given the uniqueness of the coming economic environment. Capital preservation based on empirical evidence and the realisation of exactly what money printing aims to achieve should place SWAG assets in focus.

For investors, billionaires, insurance companies and the millions of ordinary people who have assets in a pension fund or savings account, it is time to consider adding an allocation of money to assets that aim to provide robustness to a portfolio during the coming period when such robustness may prove to be essential. To my mind, that makes an allocation to SWAG assets necessary.

Summary Chapter 19

- Economic shocks happen all the time. Predicting specific shocks is often very hard to do. However, anticipating that such shocks happen is sensible. Although one can never be sure of the nature of any impending shock, one can attempt to make a portfolio as robust as possible to such potential upheavals.

- Indeed, many would argue that robustness is one of the most critical components of a portfolio. Yet, many of those who espouse such thinking still manage to construct financial portfolios that are anything but robust.

- The economic nature of the coming decade is likely to be unlike anything seen before. A confluence of factors, coming together at the same time, will make the economic outlook more difficult to predict. However, the outlook is not only likely to be more difficult to predict, it will also most likely be more volatile too.

- Constructing a portfolio for the coming decade, then, is fraught with potential problems. The need for robustness is likely to be key. In such an environment, SWAG assets are likely to provide protection to the average portfolio. SWAG assets have shown a remarkable ability to boost returns and lower volatility during the last decade, and could potentially do the same for the coming decade.

Alternative SWAGs

Asset	SWAG DNA	Swag rating
Platinum	Platinum has all of the qualities of SWAG. It also has the added advantage of having an industrial use. Platinum coins and bars can readily be found. Platinum can be held through Exchange Traded Funds (ETFs) that are readily available to investors.	*****
Palladium	Again, palladium has many of the characteristics of SWAG. It does however have some drawbacks. Unlike the other precious metals, it is actually quite hard to find palladium in a form that can be held physically. It is typically kept in granular form as this is how it gets used in industry. It can be held through ETFs.	***

Continued

Asset	SWAG DNA	Swag rating
Farmland	Just because an asset is not a SWAG does not mean that it does not have attractive investment qualities. Farmland clearly has many attractive qualities attached to it, yet it most categorically is not a SWAG. It is neither transportable nor essentially free of debt. Most land that is owned will tend to have a mortgage claim against it. Likewise, because land cannot be packed up and transported away, it is far more likely to be taxed by a government seeking to expropriate wealth.	*
Copper	Copper shares many SWAG qualities but would only ever be a fringe SWAG. The sheer size of copper that would need to be stored to be of any value would make it difficult to store. It can be owned via ETFs. Unlike gold and silver, copper would not be viewed as a form of hard currency. For these reasons it would only ever be a fringe SWAG and inferior to silver on most issues.	**
Rare stamps	There are a number of reputable companies now in existence offering investors the opportunity to invest in rare stamps. An academic study by Dimson & Spaenjers in 2009 entitled; 'The Investment Performance of Collectible Stamps (1900-2008)' concluded that stamps had, "an annualised return of 6.7% in nominal	****

Continued

Asset	SWAG DNA	Swag rating
	terms, or 2.7% in real terms. Rare stamps should be considered as having a number of SWAG characteristics.	
Vintage watches	It was touch and go whether wine or watches would qualify as the "W" in SWAG. The "Rolex Index" is often used by economists to evaluate how an economy's top-tier is doing. It measures the sales of Rolex watches per head of the population. Since Rolex holds its store of value well, it has become a form of money. Vintage watches, in particular, have taken on an investment grade quality with regular auctions and reasonable liquidity. Although there are many brands of watches, two have stood the test of time as qualifying as investment grade; Patek Philippe and Rolex. Watches have all the qualities of SWAG and should be considered an alternative SWAG.	****
Rare coins	A lack of liquidity may prevent large financial institutions looking at rare coins, but for the private investors, that lack of liquidity should not be a problem. Historically, rare coins have provided an excellent risk/return profile. For further information see "Rare Coins: A Distinct and Attractive Asset Class" Dr. Robert A. Brown, CFA. Rare coins are not perfect SWAGs, but like stamps and vintage watches, come close.	****

The Toxic Cocktail Mix

Government debt/GDP ratios	At the beginning of the 1980s, not one of the OECD economies had a debt to GDP ratio over 100%. According to academic research, a threshold of 90% represents a danger point beyond which economic growth becomes impaired. The latest crisis has seen this change radically. Now, one-third of all OECD economies are set to have debt ratios over 100% by 2012.
Demographics	The world is on the threshold of a demographic transformation brought about by falling fertility and rising life expectancy. Global aging promises to affect every dimension of economic, social, and political life. This is the conclusion of the June 2011 IMF report entitled "How Ready for Pensioners?" According to the OECD, the impact of the demographic effect will become increasingly pronounced from 2010 onwards.

Supply constraints	As a general trend, crude oil production has been moving sideways in a range of 71-75 million barrels per day since 2004.
	According to *"Perspectives on Global Development: Shifting Wealth"*, a publication from the OECD, the current economic and financial crisis is accelerating a longer-term structural transformation in the global economy. Their longer-term forecasts suggest that today's emerging countries are likely to account for nearly 60% of world GDP by 2030. These emerging economies are seeing their demand for raw materials rise very rapidly. China is predicted to double its crude oil usage by 2017. Persistently high and rising raw material prices will be the result.
Financial repression	Financial repression is not unique, but nor is it normal. It represents an act by government to impose an artificial ceiling on the level of interest rates so that, typically, inflation exceeds the rate of return on savings. It is the transfer of wealth from the saver to the borrower. One weapon in this toolkit is quantitative easing. Quantitative easing is an experiment. Many economies across the G20 have seen interest rates drop to generational lows approaching zero. Yet, economic growth has remained weak. Adopting QE is seen, even amongst its supporters, as a risky strategy given the potential inflationary impact that can result.

Continued

| Confluence | Usually, one of the above events takes place in isolation. One particular country sees its debt/GDP ratio rise too fast, indulges in QE and financial repression. Or, like Japan, one specific country has a specific deterioration in its demographic profile. What is unique about the current situation is that just about all of the OECD economies suffer to one extent or another from the above cocktail of factors. There is a confluence of headwinds that could amount to a perfect economic storm brewing. |

Notable Quotes

"It's going to end in a complete disaster. But we have to distinguish – the disaster may not happen for five to ten years. But we're heading into an iceberg. And, what will eventually happen is that the population will suffer very badly from inflation and declining real wages.

The establishment, including the government, will protect itself. And when everything becomes very bad and you have simultaneously a recession/depression.... Unemployment goes higher than 10%, say maybe 15%. When that doesn't improve, they'll go to war. And nobody can pay for the war so you print more and more money, and you have hyperinflation, and then the system goes.

That's why I'm telling everybody, you ought to own some land, and you ought to own some stocks and you ought to own some gold or a lot of gold and other precious metals. Because paper money and bonds are very vulnerable over the next five to ten years."

Dr. Marc Faber, legendary investment adviser

If we're going to finance budget deficits by printing money, we may have high inflation, even risk of hyperinflation in some countries. That's what happened in Germany in the 1920s during the Weimar Republic. We are having large budget deficits and increasing the public debt, we don't know whether it's going to be $5tr or $10tr of more debt. But there are only a few ways of resolving that debt problem: either you default on it as countries like Argentina did; or you use the inflation tax to wipe out the real value of the debt; or you have to raise taxes and cut government spending. Given the size of deficits, over time that's going to be a painful political choice to make."

Nouriel Roubini

"No one can know the precise level of net debt …at which the United States will lose its reputation…but a few more years like this one and we will find out"

Warren Buffett

"It is well enough that the people of the nation do not understand our banking and monetary system for, if they did, I believe there would be a revolution before tomorrow morning."

Henry Ford

"Paper money eventually goes down to its intrinsic value – zero"

Voltaire

"You have to choose (as a voter) between trusting to the natural stability of gold and the natural stability of the honesty and intelligence of the members of Government. And, with due respect for these gentlemen, I advise you, as long as the Capitalist system lasts, to vote for gold."

George Bernard Shaw

"The decrease in purchasing power incurred by holders of money due to inflation imparts gains to the issuers of money."

St. Louis Federal Reserve Bank

"If, however, a government refrains from regulations and allows matters to take their course, essential commodities soon attain a level of price out of reach of all but the rich, the worthlessness of the money becomes apparent, and the fraud upon the public can be concealed no longer."

John Maynard Keynes

"Bankers own the earth. Take it away from them, but leave them with the power to create money and control credit, and with a flick of a pen they will create enough (money) to buy it back."

Josiah Stamp, former President of the Bank of England

"With the exception only of the period of the gold standard, practically all governments of history have used their exclusive power to issue money to defraud and plunder the people."

Fredrich Hayek

"You can fool some of the people all of the time, and all of the people some of the time, and that's good enough."

Dr. Edwin Vieira, FAME Foundation Scholar

"Paper money has had the effect in your state that it will ever have, to ruin commerce, oppress the honest, and open the door to every species of fraud and injustice."

George Washington

"With the monetary system we have now, the careful saving of a lifetime can be wiped out in an eyeblink."

Larry Parks, Foundation for Advancement of Monetary Education

"Lenin is said to have declared that the best way to destroy the capitalist system was to debauch the currency. By a continuing process of inflation, governments can confiscate, secretly and unobserved, an important part of the wealth of their citizens. By this method they not only confiscate, but they confiscate arbitrarily; and, while the process impoverishes many, it actually enriches some. The sight of this arbitrary rearrangement of riches strikes not only at security, but at confidence in the equity of the existing distribution of wealth. Those to whom the system brings windfalls, beyond their deserts and even beyond their expectations or desires, become 'profiteers,' who are the object of the hatred of the bourgeoisie, whom the inflationism has impoverished, not less than of the proletariat. As the inflation proceeds and the real value of the currency fluctuates wildly from month to month, all permanent relations between debtors and creditors, which form the ultimate foundation of capitalism, become so utterly disordered as to be almost meaningless; and the process of wealth-getting degenerates into a gamble and a lottery."

"Lenin was certainly right. There is no subtler, no surer means of overturning the existing basis of society than to debauch the currency. The process engages all the hidden forces of economic law on the side of destruction, and does it in a manner which not one man in a million is able to diagnose."

John Maynard Keynes

"The world of finance hails the invention of the wheel over and over again, often in a slightly more unstable version. All financial innovation involves, in one form or another, the creation of debt secured in greater or lesser adequacy by real assets. This was true in one of the earliest seeming marvels: when banks discovered that they could print bank notes and issue them to borrowers in a volume in excess of the hard-money deposits in the banks' strong rooms. The depositors could be counted upon, it was believed or hoped, not to come all at once for their money. There was no seeming limit to the debt that could thus be leveraged on a given volume of hard cash. A wonderful thing......All crises have involved debt that, in one fashion or another, has become dangerously out of scale in relation to the underlying means of payment."

J.K. Galbraith "A Short History of Financial Euphoria"

"The few who understand the system will either be so interested from its profits or so dependent on its favours that there will be no opposition from that class."

Rothschild Brothers

"Government spending is always a "tax" burden on the American people and is never equally or fairly distributed. The poor and low-middle income workers always suffer the most from the deceitful tax of inflation and borrowing."

Congressman Ron Paul

"This crisis did not come about because we issued too little money but because we created economic growth with too much money and it was not sustainable."

Angela Merkel

"In the absence of the gold standard, there is no way to protect savings from confiscation through inflation. There is no safe store of value."

Alan Greenspan

"The government solution to a problem is usually as bad as the problem."

Milton Friedman

"The great thing to remember about gold is that it's the most valuable and most easily marketable commodity in the world. You can go to any town in the world, almost to any village, and hand over a piece of gold and get goods or services in return....And the next thing to remember, is that gold is virtually untraceable. Sovereigns have no serial numbers. If gold bars have Mint marks stamped on them the marks can be shaved off or the bar can be melted down and made into a new bar. That makes it almost impossible to check on the whereabouts of gold, or its movements round the world."

Ian Fleming, Goldfinger

About the author

Joe Roseman graduated from the University of Manchester in 1987. He joined Greenwell Montagu where he trained as an Economist. He subsequently worked at UBS and then S-E Banken where he was responsible for the bank's fixed income proprietary trading. In 1994, he joined the US hedge fund, Moore Capital Management. In 1998, Joe took over as Head of Economics at Moore Capital where he was responsible for a team covering the G10 economies.

Joe left Moore Capital in 2010 in order to pursue his own interests, including writing a book. He is married to Caroline and has one son, Gerald.

CPSIA information can be obtained at www.ICGtesting.com
Printed in the USA
BVOW011034150113

310675BV00001B/6/P

9 781781 485187